manuscript. Their help is most appreciated, as is the support given my research by the University of Northern Iowa.

My most personal debt is to the flier in our family, Lt. Col. Richard P. Klinkowitz, Wisconsin Air National Guard (Ret.). As my uncle, he has been a link not only to military flying but to an earlier generation's attitude toward its role in war. Some day I would like to write about the planes he flew, from Korean War-era fighter-bombers to the sophisticated 100-series supersonic fighters that still characterize American air power.

Three weeks ago, at a breakfast table overlooking Lough Eske in County Donegal, Ireland, I met a former pilot with the U.S. Ninth Air Force who, when I was less than a year old, flew B-26 missions from England to Germany and France. Our conversations, which filled the meals we shared that week, now form another link with narratives from this air war. Like my uncle, he is retired from the service, and I hope that, like so many German, British, French, and other fliers before him, he will write his combat memoirs of these years. My own generation and my children's generation need to know.

JEROME KLINKOWITZ

Widecombe in the Moor
Devon, England
October 1987

Jerome Klinkowitz

THEIR FINEST HOURS

The R.A.F. and the Luftwaffe in World War II

Marion Boyars
London . New York

First published in Great Britain in 1990 by
Marion Boyars Publishers Ltd
24 Lacy Road, London SW15 1NL

Distributed in Australia by Wild and Woolley Pty Ltd, Glebe, NSW

Originally published in the United States by
Iowa State University Press, Ames, Iowa, 1989

British Library Cataloguing in Publication Data

Klinkowitz, Jerome
    Their finest hours: the R.A.F. and the Luftwaffe in
    World War 2.
    1. World War 2. Air operations by Great Britain. Royal Air
    Force 2. World War 2. Air operations by Germany.
    Luftwaffe
    I. Title
    940.544941

ISBN 0–7145–2907–9 Cloth

Printed and bound by Biddles Ltd, Guildford and King's Lynn

For our family's flier,
LT. COL. RICHARD P. KLINKOWITZ,
Wisconsin Air National Guard (Ret.)

Contents

Preface

F ROM 1940 through the spring of 1945 the skies over Britain and Europe hosted an aerial combat unique in the history of warfare. While millions died below in a tragedy for which human expression still lacks the proper words, the struggle of the fliers above prompted a style of articulation unparalleled in accounts of modern warfare written before or since. Does the ability to talk and write so easily about such experiences mean that they have been simplified, falsified, or somehow structured to accommodate the impulses that send mankind to war in the first place? Or do the literary records of these battles in the sky hold a clue for understanding the way imagination confronts and responds to that most epic of challenges: how, in the context of a nation's fight for survival, an individual faces the immediate alternatives of one's own death or the death of one's foe. Historical accounts are inevitably influenced by political debate and by forces beyond reason's ability to organize; as Kurt Vonnegut — an avowed pacificist and brave soldier — has complained, the most terrible thing Hitler ever did was to make warfare respectable again. Therefore a literary study of how the pilots and air crew of World War II's European theater wrote about their experiences is in order. Whether one calls the conflict in the summer of 1940 the Battle of Britain or the Kanalkampf, whether the bomber crews who attacked Germany later in the war were "terrorflieger" or saviors of their own land, is not a matter for debate here. What is of concern in this study is how these fliers from Great Britain and the Commonwealth, France, and Belgium, as well as from Germany, wrote about the air war which dominated their lives for five years. Most were very young men at the time, in their late teens or early twenties. The lives of many who survived were forever altered by the war, and some who wrote about its earlier phases did not live to see its end. But their narratives are with us today — an amazingly extensive and diverse collection of texts — and finding what they say in common can be a remarkable reading experience, an exercise that should better equip us to make those ultimate moral judgments.

Sources for this study reach back in my own life more than thirty years, to school vacations, when the *Royal Air Force Flying Review* book club kept me supplied with volumes destined to become classics of air combat narrative. Their pages now yellowing and their jackets quaintly priced in shillings and pence, these books span a generation to the Britain and Germany of today, where the fliers of World War II have published yet another sheaf of memoirs as they retire from postwar careers. One can still order a pint at the traveler's bar of The Pheasant in Middle Wallop, Wiltshire, where the officers of John Cunningham's 604 night fighter squadron were quartered. Remind the barman of this fact and chances are he will point out an elderly gentleman across the room who not half an hour before said the same thing—only he's an old Beaufighter pilot come back for a meal and a memory at the inn that was his home in 1943. That was the year I was born, and it seems remarkable that so long after the Battle of Britain, the night fighter struggle, and the bomber offensive these pilots are still with us and they are still telling their stories. *Their Finest Hours* reviews a half-century of this literature, as far back as the prewar comments on the conflict everyone knew would come, with an eye to how these participants told their story—as indeed the gentleman at The Pheasant might tell you now if you asked.

In Cologne Prof. Manfred Pütz, one of West Germany's leading scholars of American literature, hosted my visit and spoke candidly about his native city's experience in the air war. In Devon Mr. and Mrs. Harry Palmer shared photos and memories of the war, as did Mr. and Mrs. John Richards, who walked the moors with us, pointing out the locations of old Gladiator and Spitfire bases, balloon barrages, radar sites, and, most touchingly, the crash site of a Junkers bomber, which was brought down by a Blenheim after it had attacked their hometown of Plymouth; John Richards showed us the village graveyard nearby, where the four German airmen had been buried. For several years Mrs. Judith Smith and Betty of Wooder Manor Hotel have made our stays most hospitable and homelike, helping us learn about England from the inside, as Peter Torberg has done for us in his country, Germany. Although they are not responsible for the opinions expressed in this book, which are necessarily and quite imperfectly my own, these people have given me a sense of how special were those years of struggle and of what an impressive story this epoch yields.

Wing Commander F. E. F. Prince, RAF (Ret.) helped collect additional material, and Kenneth Gangemi graciously critiqued my

Their Finest Hours

1
Their Finest Hours

How do we remember World War II? For many people the European theater of operations in World War II conjures up visions of air power in action. The limited fighting of 1939 is often characterized by the picture of a Luftwaffe Stuka dive-bomber setting its sights on a devastated Warsaw below, and when Germany's Western offensive begins in the spring of 1940 the screen of memory is filled with images of Messerschmitt fighters strafing the beach and embarking ships at Dunkirk, to be followed that summer and fall by the almost exclusively aerial combat known to Germans as the Kanalkampf and to Britons as the Battle of Britain. As the war proceeded, the stalemate of the Wehrmacht's Western Wall at the English Channel and the Allies' inability to mount a successful invasion until the last eleven months of a five and three-quarter years' struggle dictated that military conflict find its most potent expression in the air. The effectiveness of such air power has been debated since its inception, but the fact remains that in terms of image it was the most obvious activity in the conduct of the war, right through the D-Day invasion of June 6, 1944. Even then the fighter and bomber actions continued—some said hopelessly and pointlessly for both sides involved—yet all the while contributing to the mythologies of victory and defeat that have framed our understanding of the war.

In East and West Germany today, reminders of the air war are few but grim. In West Berlin the gutted ruin of the Kaiser-Wilhelm-Gedächtniskirche's main tower has been left to stand as a symbol of the city's devastation, just as in Dresden the Schloss remains unrepaired among an otherwise modernly rebuilt city center, its clock stopped at the hour when the February 13–14, 1945 bombing began. In England, while the shell of Coventry Cathedral, destroyed in the Luftwaffe attack of November 14, 1940, shares the minster's yard with its successor, consecrated in 1962, monuments to the air war are more grandly heroic, as befits the victor's role. The Royal Air Force with its pilots and crews is enshrined at the most crucial points of London's commemorated history, often in terms that suggest a phoenix rising from the ashes. The loveliest Wren church to be consumed by the Luftwaffe's flames—St. Clement Danes, set as an island amid the traffic of the Strand—was rebuilt to its original form in 1958 and dedicated to the RAF, the badges of eight hundred squadrons and units carved as slate keys and set into its pavement floor. Step into Westminster Abbey and the first memorial you see establishes the priority for all other monuments to follow. "Remember Winston Churchill," we are told, in the form of a floor stone which spells out the instructions of the Queen and Parliament given on the twenty-fifth anniversary of the Battle of Britain, September 15, 1965—a major statesman's lifetime achievement here centered on one hundred days' combat in the summer of 1940 waged by scarcely more than a thousand pilots.

Churchill's presence is ikonic, much like the solitary Spitfire left to grace the annual Battle of Britain Day flypast after its Hurricane sister and Lancaster cousin peel off—an image no less effective for its slight departure from truth (Hurricanes outnumbered Spitfires three to two in combat and in victories), since the Battle of Britain was as much symbol as substance. Churchill's oratory and the gallant Spitfire are essential parts of the story, and it is on these terms that the Battle was won. The holiest part of Westminster sanctifies this memory, as in the magnificent stained glass of the RAF Chapel the British airmen, in modern service dress and combat garb, are taken up into a medieval rendering of Heaven.

For five brief years in the twentieth century, warfare assumed a unique dimension, and telling its story became a novel art. From the first days of the Battle of Britain in 1940 through the end of the bomber offensive against Germany in 1945, a new style of combat gave fresh character to the war effort. More crucially, in a day of technologized conflict the isolation of the fighter cockpit and the close teamwork of the bomber crew restored a sense of personal mission absent from war for centuries. If Ernest Hemingway's dismay at the anonymous and often meaningless slaughter of World War I expressed disillusion with the purpose of war, the memoirs and narratives of World War II's pilots and crews established an entirely different sense of accomplishment and meaning.

At the center of their work is the art of story telling, to which the peculiarities of aerial combat were especially suited. A war's infantry, tank, and artillery battles can be counted on the fingers of a single hand; the career of the most honored naval commander may be distinguished by just one or two engagements, and the entire war may turn upon a few encounters lasting a matter of hours. But during the Battle of Britain, British and German pilots faced each other as often as three times a day for over three months, a pattern that establishes the serial structure so necessary for narrative. Later in the war British bomber crews counted their service in units of thirty missions — for the Pathfinders, fifty — and their most familiar story is the dramatic progress through their tour of operations. Each battle was a pointedly individual, man-to-man conflict, with personal tests of nerves, immediate proof of success or failure, and opportunities for chivalry unknown since the days of knightly combat. Unlike in wars before or since, each man could see what he was fighting for and could depend upon his own skills to press his cause. Their battles fulfilled the narrative unities of time, place, and action as could no other branch of modern warfare. And so it is no accident that their stories quickly became the myths and ikons of the new war.

As stories, they organized their nations' sense of what the war meant and how it was progressing. From the diving Stuka bomber over Warsaw to the Messerschmitt prowling across the Channel from airfields occupied in France, the Luftwaffe became the symbol of Hitler's successfully bold aggression, while the RAF's Spitfire served as Churchill's ready-made image for the dogged defiance by a brave, outnumbered few. The situation map was clear for all to see, with arrows thrusting into southeast England from Belgium and France, representing the challenge from German bombers and fighters with little need for metaphor. As for the British pilots, their role in the narrative was tailored for a prime minister's rousing speech, a stylistic figure more than adequate to sway the House of Commons, the British people themselves, and even an America pondering the wisdom of its continued allegiance and aid.

Fifty years after the event the Battle of Britain may well be regarded as a more effective story than as a completely successful engagement of military aviation. The tactical goals of neither side were achieved — Germany did not invade England nor take her out of the war, but neither was the Luftwaffe's power defeated, as Hitler simply established his Western Wall at the Channel and turned to expand eastward, the goal he set forth in *Mein Kampf*. German historians themselves do not recognize that a "battle of Britain" took place, suggesting instead that aerial harassment and the threat of a seaborne invasion were ploys to force an armistice so that the Wehrmacht could undertake its real business with the Soviet Union. But from the British point of view the whole image of the war was at stake. Nearly a year of hostilities had gone by without an Allied success. England looked as weak as its French and Low Country neighbors had been, and U.S. ambassador Joseph Kennedy was advising his president that America should abandon Great Britain as an ally and insure its own peace (on better terms) with Hitler. There was even doubt among the British people how much resolve was left to fight.

That the writers accomplished their task is undebatable. Although the RAF lost an unacceptable number of pilots, the Battle of Britain was counted as a major success; its standoff nature allowed the Air Ministry to inflate Luftwaffe losses to thrice their actual total, winning a major propaganda victory with Britain's allies and rallying morale at home. Bomber Command gained a similar symbolic victory by striking almost at once against the enemy with the only offensive weapon available, the long-range bomber—the only type of aircraft the Germans lacked and against which they were slow to prepare effective defensive tactics. That 90 percent of the bombers sent on missions to the Ruhr in 1941 failed to get within five miles of their target was irrelevant, since even the much more accurate attacks that followed did not have a significant effect on Germany's ability to wage war until midway through 1944 (according to Air Chief Marshal Sir Arthur Harris, head of Bomber Command from 1942 onwards). On the German side, Luftwaffe memoirists such as Adolf Galland and Werner Baumbach record their service's early flushes of success, followed by a slow but steady attrition of purpose due to misconstrued strategy and political interference. Indeed, the stories of their respective air forces invite the pilots to see the story of the air war in classically narrative terms, as neatly balanced as a seesaw: on one end the RAF, fighting for its very existence throughout the 1920s and 1930s, its ninety-six World War I squadrons reduced to an operational ten by May 1919 and thereafter threatened with absorption into the army or navy; on the other end the Luftwaffe, carefully and generously nurtured in secret and then unveiled in 1935 as the symbol of Germany's new pride and aggressiveness. The Battle of Britain tipped the seesaw the other way, as England rallied behind its perceived saviors while Hitler and Göring began tampering with Luftwaffe tactics, their improvisations driving such young commanders as Galland and Baumbach to despair.

In the air, however, the personalities of British and German fliers were much the same, even though there was a great range of characters fighting and then writing about their exploits. Douglas Bader, in Paul Brickhill's *Reach for the Sky,* and Adolf Galland, in his own *The First and the Last,* are both portrayed as self-proclaimed knights, who battle their leaders as often as they do their enemies, pure Lancelots of a style of combat that they themselves had to invent as it happened. Galland befriended Bader, his British victim, in 1941, and the two became close friends after the war. This pattern was repeated by Group Captain Peter Townsend and Unteroffizier Karl Missy, Wing Commander Bob Braham and Leutnant Robert Spreckels, and countless other adversaries whose few seconds on opposite ends of each other's machine guns and cannon led to lifelong friendships once hostilities had ceased. In a classic literary interaction, Spreckels even wrote the preface to Braham's *"Scramble!",* and Bader supplied the foreword to Hans Rudel's *Stuka Pilot* as a result of meeting this German ace during his tour of British airfields in June 1945, barely a month after the last shots were fired. These alliances were based on far more than irony or good sportsmanship; throughout the war British and German aircrews exhibited an extraordinary amount of mutual respect and even kinship, with the rare unchivalrous airman quickly ostracized by his colleagues as the real enemy.

In the five decades since World War II began, over one hundred artistically significant personal accounts of the European air war have appeared in English. From Richard Hillary's *The Last Enemy* (1942) to Peter Townsend's *Duel in the Dark* (1986) and Ron Smith's *Rear Gunner Pathfinders* (1987), these works are distinguished by a high sense of literary purpose and an uncommonly even judgment toward their subject—a judgment which either resists or deftly accommodates to its own view the revisions of military history. Unlike memoirs written by the fighters of other wars before and since, there is no first, second, or third wave of reaction following the currents of political thought. Although Great Britain has undergone a major transformation in response to such forces of change as postwar austerity and the welfare state, the loss of empire, the Cold War, and the Suez and the Falkland Islands wars, its "story" of air combat has remained essentially unchanged; the recurrent pictures of Churchill and the Spitfire, the gallant few scrambling to the skies at daybreak, and the all-suffering bomber crews flying through hellish destruction night after night have survived all temptations to correct them to a more historical sense of truth. Germany, whose postwar history is perhaps more orderly (as a slow but steady growth from destruction) but no less spectacular in terms of accumulative change, also relies upon a consistent attitude in its Luftwaffe chronicles—from the humiliation of Versailles, through the development of a secret air force via gliding clubs and bases in Russia, to the early lightning successes confounded by self-defeating tactics in the war's closing years. Each is a narrative that served an important purpose in wartime and immediately after the war, and in nearly five decades of writing no author has dared tamper with its structure.

That very structure, however, has engendered the success of the air memoir as a literary form no less durable than the Cavalier sonnet or even the classical epic. Individual heroism and larger national purpose are conjoined so effectively, in such works as J. E. Johnson's *Wing Leader* and Paul Brickhill's *The Dam Busters* and *Reach for the Sky,* that the responsibilities of epic are served as a country is brought to understand and rally to its mission. Such German works as Wilhelm Johnen's *Duel Under the Stars* and Heinz Knoke's *I Flew for the Führer,* each of which had great success in English translation, could not only provide a foil to the RAF's achievement but could explain the motivations and disappointments of the equally gallant Luftwaffe pilots. Which was exactly what the readers of these works demanded, for from the hop fields of Kent in 1940 and the embattled German cities in 1943 and 1944 the airmen's contrails and tracer fire sketched a dramatic and observable narrative, which lent meaning and purpose to an otherwise irrational war.

The most common trait of these wartime memoirs is for the British pilots to view their experiences in terms of literary rather than historical structures—for, unlike the Luftwaffe crews, theirs is a story of valorized success, whereas the German accounts read like a chronicle of historical inexorability. An RAF veteran typically begins his story not with his first interest in flying or his entry into the service, or even with the outbreak of war and his first missions, but rather with an account of the day he was shot down—a heroic gesture, for history will insure his eventual victory and personal success. Richard Hillary's *The Last Enemy* opens with an ominous scramble over the Thames estuary, the thrill of combat jinxed by a jammed cockpit hood, which worries him before the mission and serves as the key element of his near destruction. Unable to escape the flames devouring his wounded Spitfire, Hillary suffers disabling burns, from which it will take him the full length of his memoir to recover. He finally comes to terms with his injury and his role in the war when he faces the terror of civilian casualties during a London air raid; a dying woman sees his scarred face and says, "I see they got you too" (p. 178).

This same full-circle technique distinguishes Bob Braham's *"Scramble!"* and Geoff Taylor's *Piece of Cake,* the stories of a Mosquito pilot whose operations ended in a dogfight over Denmark and a Lancaster pilot who was shot down over Hanover by a night fighter and spent nearly three years as a prisoner of war. Braham's approach is to begin with his final combat on June 25, 1944, then return to his first experience with flying and work his way forward to a more complete and hence understandable account of his last battle. Taylor's technique is almost entirely metaphorical. Since he spends most of the war in a German prison camp, he can escape the local determinations of history only by transforming the event into one "long day," which begins with a soggy hangover and a vexing mission and ends with his repatriation three years later. Peter Townsend's massive *Duel of Eagles,* which details the histories of the RAF and the Luftwaffe from World War I through the Battle of Britain, starts in medias res, on February 3, 1940, with the successful combat in which Townsend becomes the first to bring down a German bomber on English soil since 1918. This coincidence alone unites Townsend's personal experience with the larger historical chronicle. But he also takes advantage of a next-day meeting with a surviving German crewman to begin a lifelong friendship and to research their common histories, which throughout the book are carefully paralleled from childhood through adolescent interests in flight to their deadly encounter over Whitby.

In telling their stories, airmen of both nations (as well as Polish, Czech, and French airmen in expatriate squadrons) habitually dress up their self-consciously literary structures with artistic language and conceits. Taking off from Spilsby on his fateful mission, Geoff Taylor pauses to note the force of Lancasters, Halifaxes, and Stirlings forming up over Mablethorpe: "As they banked and climbed, the last of the daylight glinted on their wings and on the bright perspex of turrets and cockpits until, as if appalled at the sight, the sun slipped abruptly over the horizon" (*Piece of Cake,* p. 24). Waiting across the Channel is Luftwaffe night fighter pilot Wilhelm Johnen, whose *Duel Under the Stars* describes combats which might well include the bagging of Taylor's bomber above Hanover. He too sees the war in images, almost as a movie whose course of action he need initiate by firing his guns:

Shall I give him another burst I wondered, drawing closer. But the enemy was badly hit and the greedy flames were glowing eerily in the darkness, lighting up the red, white and blue circles. We were now flying close to the enemy, watching what would happen. One of the crew bailed out. For the fraction of a second his body gleamed in the light of the flames before he fell into the yawning depths. One after another followed suit and eight men all bailed out. It was high time, for a moment later the port petrol tank exploded and the machine hurtled to the ground, leaving behind it a long fiery tail. I did an aileron turn and watched the grandiose sight of the crashing Lancaster. The comet streaked down to the earth and disappeared through the bank of clouds. A few seconds later a column of flame lit up the night. This was the first kill of the night. (p. 138)

In fact, there are many reminders that what appears to be the spectator's seat is not all so secure. Sneaking up behind another Lancaster, Johnen explodes the bomber's fuel tanks with his first shots, and his crew "insisted that they could feel the heat of the explosion in their cockpits" (p. 100). When Peter Townsend's Hurricane is discovered in a similar position beneath a Dornier, the belly-gunner opens up on him so abruptly that Townsend swears he can hear the firing of the gun. A common reaction is the feeling of participating in a show and witnessing it at the same time, as Johnen remarks when flying into a major raid on Berlin:

Berlin defended itself magnificently. The brightly lit night was dotted with thousands of flak bursts up to 24,000 feet. I flew right into a salvo and was flung about the sky by the blast. But I got through. Right and left, above and below me, burning machines rocketed earthwards. Countless fires had sprung up below. Damaged night-fighters fired their distress signals, enemy bombers exploded in the air, spraying the city with a bright-coloured rain of gleaming confetti. A grandiose fireworks display. The constant bursting of flak shells tortured my nerves. The acrid stench of gunpowder entered the cockpit. (p. 104)

British night fighter pilots such as Peter Townsend and John Cunningham, and even bomber pilots such as Guy Gibson flying a courier plane from one base to another, would view the London inferno in similar terms. Townsend in particular incorporates the war-time diary of an East Ender to show how devastating this bombing could be, and Johnen takes care to describe the firestorms that destroyed Hamburg and Dresden. But the fighter pilot sees the earth from the perspective of a world unto itself, and a frequently indulged thought is of the godlike view one enjoys from on high, as Johnen remarks on a clear night over central Germany:

> In such weather at 15,000 to 18,000 feet the pilot has a field of some 350 miles. Flying over Hanover, for example, I could see the Hamburg flak in action, bombs dropping on Berlin, fires in Leipzig and incendiaries falling on Cologne. Between these cities I could see the gleaming network of searchlight cones and the square markers of night-fighter airfields. For the German night fighter, the Homeland was an open book which he had no difficulty in reading. (Johnen, pp. 101–2)

The range of Johnen's view indicates another difference between the literary natures of the most typical RAF and Luftwaffe accounts. Whereas the Germans are always on the move (the picture of a worn-out boot, suggesting the unit's nomadic wanderings from base to base across the length and breadth of Europe, graced the fuselages of one Messerschmitt Jagdstaffel), whether assaulting England from occupied airfields in the West or later scrambling about the homeland to intercept any number of different bomber raids, the RAF is more firmly attached to its home bases, where a pilot officer might breakfast on marmalade and tea with his wife in a vine-covered cottage, fly a combat sortie over the Channel or the Continent that afternoon, then drink with his colleagues at the local pub until closing time. Not even the debacle of Dunkirk could disorder this sense of domestic tranquility—with the battered survivors landing on the quays at Dover, French soldier Michel Nastorg found half of the English there walking around with tennis rackets and golf clubs, while Flight Lieutenant Al Deere, his battle dress in rags after being shot down over the embarkation and brought home on a destroyer, was nearly thrown off a train to London for lacking a ticket. Yet even the combatants held on to this sense of the status quo in Britain, barely twenty-two miles from the raging battle at Dunkirk. Bomber pilot Guy Gibson, on leave in Brighton, had to break off his stroll along the seaside promenade when a flight of strafing Messerschmitts bore down upon the holidaymakers.

Fighting from a base so close to home has its ironies, but the bomber crews preferred to exploit the situation's lyrical dimensions. Even an airfield tucked away in the Lincolnshire wolds soon develops its own familiar character, and navigator Don Charlwood carefully rehearses its features throughout his memoir, *No Moon Tonight,* so that the reader can share, in an intimately literary sense, the experience of flying from such a place. More than one narrative features the rallying point of Lincoln Cathedral, bomber crews sighting its cruciform shape before turning off on their unholy missions over Germany. But Charlwood strives for more poetic effect as he walks with his Waaf girlfriend beneath the airfield's signal beacon one night, and the next sees it fade behind him as his Lancaster climbs toward the North Sea and its target in the Ruhr: "The darkness suddenly engulfed her and Essen engulfed me. In a moment it was beyond belief that she had been so near" (p. 102). Flying home on his last of thirty operations, a particularly difficult raid over Duisburg, Charlwood makes the last fifty miles go faster by counterpointing the interchange of commands with his thoughts of Joan at the moment and the words they will exchange on his return. Such paralleling is a familiar literary device in these memoirs, sometimes comic—as in Jack Currie's hilarious interpolation of Air Vice-Marshal Bennett's solemn V-E Day address with the squadron members' clowning in ranks. But the best effect is the purely dramatic sense of working as a crew member—plotting course, watching for flak and fighters, calling for evasive maneuvers, making the bomb run and turning for home, all of which Don Charlwood supplies in rapid-fire dialogue paced with passing comments on the scene. The Lancaster's crew of seven forms a manageable dramatis personae, with a clearly defined role for each character, the sum of which spans the complex experience of flying a thirty-ton, bomb-laden machine.

Memoirs such as *Lancaster Target, Mosquito Victory,* and *No Moon Tonight,* although written more than twenty-five years apart (and think how much the world has changed from 1956 to 1983), present consistent and vivid accounts of the close, intimate world a bomber crew shared. A fighter pilot may be alone within his own perspective, but the seven members of a Lancaster crew (eight when a second pilot was added for training) share their own small society aloft at the same altitudes, from which one world, friendly, loyal, and secure, could look down upon an altogether different environment where chaos reigned supreme. Jack Currie's comrades maintain their dramatic roles even outside of combat; when an American B-17 makes an emergency landing at their base, Currie describes the evening in play form, complete with dialogue and stage directions. But the real drama is aloft. The transformation can be one of space, as a mission in *Lancaster Target* shows:

> on this occasion, we burst out of the cloud into an open sky, and the whole expanse of the Lüneberg Heath spread 20,000 feet below. As the last time we had seen the ground was over Lincolnshire three hours before, the effect was startling. I felt as though I had woken in the middle of the night, and opened my eyes to find that my bedstead and I had been lifted into outer space while I was sleeping. (p. 78)

Time and space can dance together under the pilot's control to create an entirely new dimension of mastery over the earth's rotation, as Currie describes just a page later:

> Then I would loosen my straps, engage the automatic pilot, sit back and really enjoy that cigarette. At those moments, cruising home on half power with the darkness, while the dawn began to touch the sky behind my left shoulder with a few bright strokes of gold, the crew cocooned in warm leather and fur, lulled by the gently throbbing metal, the terrors of the night would soon disperse. A few hundred miles ahead lay the coast of England, beyond it the Lincolnshire fields, breakfast and bed. The next briefing seemed a long way off.
>
> Between the passing night and the emerging day the bomber floated, steady and secure. I could, if I wished, for a time postpone the dawn: push down the nose, lose enough height to mask the daylight with the eastern horizon, and it would still be yesterday. (p. 79)

The most remarkable feature of Bomber Command memoirs is the writers' ability to empathize with their enemies, not just on the ground but even in the air, at the very target the Germans are bombing. Here the literary talent of projecting oneself into the role of another person overcomes all hostility and animosity, for the world of shared routine and risk is closer to the crewmen than any political issues. Don Charlwood recounts such a scene with particular effect. On a night's leave, as he listens to an opera broadcast from German-occupied Poland, he hears in the distance the antiaircraft guns open up along the Humber estuary; soon his hotel's garden is illuminated by the searchlights now scanning the skies. "High up," he notes, "I could hear the drone of an aircraft, tortured and afraid. Knowing only the terror of air crew, my heart was with the pilot carrying out his lone task against extreme odds." The drama unfolds quickly, as the searchlights capture the plane, "small as a moth and beautifully silvered," as it dives and turns in the flak. Soon the firing ends and the night returns to normal. "I went inside and resumed listening to Mozart, wondering what manner of man had died" (p. 130).

Ultimately, these stories come down to a very personal contest that pits one man against individual foes and the larger nature of the battle, but also tests his estimate of himself. The fighter pilot must combat not just Messerschmitts and Focke-Wulfs but such elemental forces as gravity and the destructive potential of his own machine. Spitfire and Hurricane pilots in particular lead madly indefinite lives, one moment lounging in the fragrant grass of a southeast England airfield in the bloom of high summer—an experience Peter Townsend more than once compares to being a member of the finest flying club in the world, as many of his fellow pilots were before the war—and the next moment hurtling about the sky at four hundred miles per hour in a machine ready at any time to explode or burn or be torn apart by cannon fire. The bomber crew's life is more orderly since its operations are planned half a day in advance and are limited in number to thirty, even though the casualty rate of 5 percent makes the completion of a tour statistically unlikely. Plotting those thirty missions yields a structure not unlike that of a suspense novel of thirty chapters, but in this case there is no guarantee that the hero will live through Chapter 1. Yet even when the seemingly impossible is achieved and a memoirist like Jack Currie or Don Charlwood sets out on his final operation, there is the sad sense of finishing an enjoyable and important book. As Charlwood confesses, "Perhaps anything we are doing for the last time we do with regret, or, if not regret, with sharp memories of all the times that have gone before. Perhaps thus we acknowledge our mortality" (p. 156).

If the individual exploits of pilots and crews yield the particulars of literary activity, it is the epic nature of their cumulative air battles that lends their tale its larger structure. For both the British and the German air forces World War II divides itself into three movements of large-scale aerial action. First and foremost is the Battle of Britain, when during the three and a half months from July 10 through October 31, 1940, the RAF struggled to repulse Luftwaffe attacks on coastal convoys, ports, airfields, factories, and eventually London itself. Here the ikons are the Spitfire and Messerschmitt, the key players such identifiable air aces as Bader and Galland, and the theme Air Chief Marshal Dowding's brilliant "generalcy of the air" (as Churchill put it), that is, his direction of the RAF's meager resources against a Luftwaffe onslaught that continually defeated itself through tactical error and strategic mismanagement. Although at this stage of the conflict German planes and crews outnumbered the British three to one, key elements of "the story" contribute to the feeling that the RAF is destined to be a winner, even though from a strictly military standpoint the Battle of Britain was not a significant battle at all. First, the RAF was extremely vulnerable in 1938; after years of neglect, at the time of the Munich crisis it was deplorably weak and as easy a target for the Luftwaffe as the Polish, French, Dutch, and Belgian air forces would prove to be. Its year's reprieve, however, allowed for squadron strength to be rebuilt and for the Hurricane and Spitfire to come into service and replace the biplane fighter, which had been the RAF's mainstay since World War I. Another nine months of the relatively uneventful "phoney war" provided time for training and staffing. But even after the Battle of Britain began, strategy and tactics had to be reinvented for this new style of aerial warfare. Unlike the Germans, who had developed techniques appropriate for their high-speed equipment during the Spanish Civil War, the RAF was still using line-astern formations, which only the pressures of battle would modify into the more workable finger four (in which two pairs of wingmen would cooperatively cover the sky). At Fighter Command and at Group headquarters another battle was being fought: first, to conserve dwindling resources during the battle of France (a struggle Dowding won with Churchill and the war cabinet), and second, over whether separate squadron attacks should yield to larger, more concentrated "big wings" (an argument, favored by Group Commander Trafford Leigh-Mallory and his ace pilot Douglas Bader, which eventually cost Dowding his job). Yet even though over five hundred pilots and one thousand British aircraft were lost — an unacceptable number considering the limited supply of each, and fatal had Göring not changed his strategy at the brink of victory — and Air Chief Marshal Dowding was ingloriously replaced, both the RAF and its Fighter Command leader emerge as victors, simply because the longer book of history proves them right. Had the second and third chapters of aerial warfare proceeded differently, the Battle of Britain would be another story altogether.

The calculatedly defensive role of the night fighter forms the second major chapter of aerial warfare and makes a strong narrative

15

transition from the Battle of Britain to the war above Germany. Although the RAF had experimented with nighttime interceptions earlier in 1940, it was Göring's decision in September to bomb London and the provincial cities by darkness that forced the issue and accelerated development of both tactics and equipment. Here again there is the classic story of a struggle against long odds, although here those odds are determined by science and the visual limitations of night. Early attempts were made to train single pilots in Hurricanes for nighttime interceptions with the aid of ground control, searchlights, the full moon, and even "cat's eyes" talents. In a more sophisticated method, radar observers (converted from their old job of rear gunner) guided their pilots to the prey in two-man, twin-engine aircraft. Because of the dramatic structure of a well-coordinated crew not just triumphing over the enemy but mastering complex and rapidly developing technology, and also because of the pathos involved in a handful of men venturing forth into the darkness, that dread childhood enemy, to defend their utterly vulnerable English cities below, the Blenheim-Beaufighter-Mosquito story is more successful than the few tales of Hurricanes muddling around in the dark. Whereas in *Duel in the Dark,* Peter Townsend remains his own man, as much the lone eagle as in his earlier book about day fighting in the Battle of Britain, pilot-observer teams such as John Cunningham and C. F. Rawnsley, Bob Braham and Henry Jacobs, and Jack Currie and Norman Pittam exploit the full breadth of physical contrasts, differing yet complementary personalities, class distinctions, and even contrary attitudes toward the war. Their stories mark an important advance over the fighter narratives, just as the night fighter saga that runs from 1940 to the end of the war matures and deepens as planes improve in performance, radar interception devices are perfected, and pilot-observer teams sharpen their collaborative technique. The night fighter mission itself grows from a relatively hopeless gesture against the blitzing Luftwaffe to a crack force against whom no foe can be secure, even within the bomber stream over Germany or among their own planes in the landing circuit of their French and German bases. The night fighter story is in fact the most historically accurate chapter in the air war, where literary expression and military fact find a common structure for events reaching from the RAF's failure to repulse the London bombings in the fall of 1940 to the last raids over Germany in the spring of 1945. And like all structures it is perfectly reversible in effect, since the German night fighter pilot is able to invert his foe's Battle of Britain mystique to view his side as struggling in dwindling numbers against insurmountable odds; yet he himself shows great bravery and no small cunning as he retards for a moment what in this style of narrative must be the unavoidable historical conclusion. Despite these qualities, the night fighter story is the least known narrative of the war and has been overshadowed by the knightly heroics of Battle of Britain fighter combat and the apocalyptic inferno of Bomber Command.

And an inferno is what the bomber story is, in both metaphor and theme, as pilots and crews struggle not only with their nerve-breaking missions through flak and fighters but with the moral consequence of their acts. If the Battle of Britain Window in Westminster Abbey—with its anachronistic but effective mixture of saints and divinities in time-of-Christ garb welcoming to Heaven dress-blue airmen looking like they have just stepped from a Spitfire cockpit, parade review, or the station's local pub—sets the tone for the fighter conflict of 1940, Bomber Command's memorials are the gutted ruins left to stand in both England and Germany as a record of the war's devastation. Next to the new Coventry Cathedral stand the scarred walls of the old minster's bombed-out shell, just as the stalagmitic rubble of the Kaiser-Wilhelm-Gedächtniskirche reminds Berlin of its 6,427 acres of total destruction from Allied bombing.

Yet for all the chaos that its mission wrought, the Bomber Command story is by far the most easily organized. Unlike Fighter Command, whose strategy and tactics did not exist before 1936 and whose methods were in disarray throughout the Battle of Britain—even as the action was won—Bomber Command profited from extensive study of bombing strategy and tactics by both military thinkers and politicians, such as the Italian general Giulio Douhet, whose early work pioneered the concepts of strategic civilian bombing, and British prime minister Stanley Baldwin, who directed government policy with the dictum that "the bomber will always get through." In the 1930s bomber production had priority, thanks to an understanding that since fighters (certainly as they existed in 1936) could never hope to even decimate an attacking bomber force, the only effective defense would be preemptive bomber strikes against enemy airfields, factories, and population centers to eradicate its ability to wage war. Unlike the scrambles and sweeps of fighter tactics, such bombing offensives lend themselves to mapped-out campaigns plottable by month, day, and hour. Sir Arthur Harris's *Bomber Offensive* is an orderly story of mounting numbers and success rates, subject only to the interference of the other services with the grand strategy of victory from the air.

On the German side, Werner Baumbach's *Broken Swastika* traces an equally consistent decline of Luftwaffe forces and of the German will to fight on. The bomber crews themselves do not experience anything like the maniacal fighter station life of the Battle of Britain or the night fighters' uncertain forays into darkness with faulty instruments, for every man has been exquisitely trained in a skill—piloting, navigating, bomb aiming, or gunnery—and follows a schedule of operations posted in advance for a finite thirty missions. Of all styles of fighting, bombing is the least uncertain, for crews know where the worst flak is and how to avoid it, when they can expect to find night fighters prowling in the bomber stream, and which cities put up the stiffest defense. On the other hand, their role is by far the most fatalistic, as there can be no deviation from the target and the bomb run must be made for a steady twenty seconds through the hellfire of enemy defense. All these factors make for a special story, in which the adventures of combat can be measured against a steady accrual of data: for Harris, how many tons dropped and how many acres devastated; for the crews, how many missions completed on their countdown to thirty.

As for the moral subtext, the Bomber Command stories yield the broadest range of reactions. Some writers, notably the night fighter pilots who had little success defending London in 1940, justify their actions on the basis of historical precedent—the German bombing of London in 1915, to which Peter Townsend refers time and again and which Churchill employed to great rhetorical effect in the House of Commons. The London blitz itself was a more timely argument, from Air Chief Marshal Harris's prophetic words uttered during an early attack—"They are sowing the wind"—to his strategists' careful study and adaptation of Luftwaffe techniques for the RAF's own campaign against Hamburg, Berlin, and the Ruhr. Bomber crews themselves wrestled with the abstractness of their role—to dump tons of high explosives and incendiaries on very real men, women, and children yet from a conscience-effacing altitude of four miles or more. Ironically, they viewed their own risk as an abstract mathematical average rather than as a real chance of being hit by flak or gunfire. Area versus precision bombing had been debated before the war and into its early phases both within the RAF and between the British and American strategists, with Bomber Command finding its best reasons for indiscriminate attacks after high losses forced it into a nighttime role (when precision bombing was impossible). Yet enough crews had reservations about this style of slaughter to provide motivation for joining the Pathfinders, a special group whose accurate target marking made bombing by night a somewhat more noble affair. For their peace of conscience the Pathfinders paid a high price — fifty operations rather than thirty and a higher rate of attrition. But for some it was the only bearable choice, and herein lies another story inspiring the best literary expression.

The aerial combat by hundreds of thousands of young men over Britain and Europe during the Second World War is remembered as their finest hours not simply because of what they did but how they did it. And fashioning that "how" is the business of a high style of literary writing never so finely concentrated in any other aspect of modern warfare. For each aspect of the conflict there is a story — of men, machines, tactics, philosophies, and even national histories. The legless pilot Bader, having more trouble with the service than with his own disability as he struggles to get back into action; the brilliant designer Mitchell, overspending his failing health in order to give Britain the Spitfire fighter it needs to triumph; Beaverbrook, performing miracles to build and repair these machines; Dowding, pledged to save his dwindling fighter resources even as the prime minister and his cabinet were pledging them to France; Harris, working to insure a bomber offensive that would wreak destruction unrivaled until Hiroshima — all these stories are personal yet of epic consequence. And the leaders themselves are as grandly individual and characterizable as the protagonists of any vivid story, from the doughty Churchill to the flamboyant and sometimes reckless Göring.

This cast of characters, all with sharply defined roles played off against each other as foils, enact their drama on a closely circumscribed stage, a geographically historical area whose canopy of sky can be scanned by one man's view. From the Pas de Calais, Göring and his generals can watch the cliffs of Dover as they select their next target of aggression; from the airfields of southeast England RAF pilots and ground observers can see and hear the Luftwaffe bomber fleets forming up over France. From fifteen thousand feet a German night fighter can witness every corner of his country in flames, and late in the war early risers in Lincolnshire can see the trails of V-2 rockets rising over Holland in the dawn. In 1940 and 1941 the German bombers flew westward across the Channel in an eerie reprise of the Norman Invasion nearly nine hundred years before, only to be repulsed and replaced by an eastward tide of fire and destruction that would shape world politics for the next half-century and more.

Few conflicts of international consequence have been played out by such a limited cast of characters within such finite and observable bounds of time and space. Limits are usually imposed afterward by poets, dramatists, and fiction writers seeking to reduce the war to imaginatively understandable form. But because these battles were conceived and executed in a conscious imitation of literary structure, the RAF's and Luftwaffe's stories come to us already made as art. There is no doubt that the participants had this role in mind, for diarists recorded their adventures with the noble sense of Crusaders, and their leaders reacted to the unfolding events as high drama.

Viewing the onslaught of the first massive Luftwaffe attacks on Göring's *Adlertag* ("Eagle Day") from Number 11 Group Operations Room at Uxbridge, with Group Commander Keith Park in attendance and the action board spread out before him like a living map, Churchill could witness in grandly dramatic form the outnumbered British squadrons fighting off and then decimating their German adversaries. Driving back to his residence at Chequers that night, the prime minister reflected on his commanders' genius and his pilots' bravery that day and cautioned his aide not to disturb him, as he was deep in thought. "Don't speak to me," Churchill told him, "I've never been so moved." And as their drive continued, the great man was heard to murmur, "Never in the field of human conflict was so much owed . . . ." In terms such as these have their finest hours been recorded and told again for posterity.

2
The Quest

O N October 16, 1939, Great Britain received its first hostile fire of World War II—as almost all of it would be, from the sky. At 2:15 in the afternoon a flight of nine Junkers 88 bombers led by Hauptmann Helmut Pohle made landfall on the east coast of Scotland just above the Firth of Forth, aiming for the cruisers *Edinburgh* and *Southampton* at anchor off the Forth Bridge. Waiting at ten thousand feet was a section of Spitfires from the 602 City of Glasgow Squadron, which at twenty-two minutes after the hour was ordered to investigate unconfirmed sightings of a formation heading toward the Firth. Beneath them on this splendid fall day the people of Scotland were strolling the seaside and the golf links, oblivious to the "phoney war" that for over a month and a half had been conducted without any action on the western front. But soon there was action aplenty, as two Spitfires zeroed in on Pohle's machine, shot off his cabin roof, and knocked out both engines, sending it down across the waterfront at Kirkcaldy and giving the town's promenaders a grandstand view.

Across the Firth at Dalkeith another section of 602's fighters spotted a solitary Heinkel 111 heading toward Edinburgh on a reconnaissance mission and turned quickly for the kill. The war was quickly brought home to Scotland, as Douglas McRoberts describes in *Lions Rampant:*

> The three Spitfires closed, in line astern formation, as the Heinkel dived and turned for the coast. Golfers on a course below looked up in astonishment as the great, black machine blasted over them, followed by the snarling fighters. Then they dived for cover as a cascade of cartridge cases and belt links rained down from the Spitfires' wings—and, suddenly, they'd gone, the sound of straining aero engines and chattering machine guns echoing across the course. (p. 58)

Four months later the first German bomber was brought down over England itself in circumstances that command the same style of description, from the German crews' departure from base, through the aerial combat, to the crashing machine's abrupt intrusion into the daily routine of life below. On February 3, 1940, Peter Townsend's Hurricane intercepted a Heinkel 111 menacing naval targets off Whitby—by Hitler's order Luftwaffe planes were still avoiding land targets—and soon the author of *Duel of Eagles* was on the attack:

> Then I was firing at [German crewmen] Missy, Wilms, Leushake, and Meyer, who at Schleswig only a few hours before had been shoveling snow and enjoying coffee and sandwiches. It never occurred to me at the time that I was killing men. I saw only a big Heinkel with black crosses on it. But in that Heinkel Peter Leushake was already dead and Johann Meyer, his stomach punctured by bullets, mortally wounded.

The bomber turns for shore, and Townsend follows his victim as it skims the cliffs at Whitby and passes over housetops: "A girl heard the screaming of sea gulls and then the Heinkel seemed to be passing in front of her window" (p. 205).

As the stricken plane blunders inland, more people of England are brought into the war: teenagers and old age pensioners who see the plane roar by and chase it to the crash site, an old woman at a bus stop who can see the pilot through the cockpit window as it passes low overhead, and finally the villagers at Bannial Flat Farm who with great tenderness and pity try to rescue the crew from the wreckage. The scene is pathos personified, even to the youngster who finds a trail of red spots in the snow; as Townsend reveals, "It was blood which had dripped from the Heinkel as it came in to land" (p. 207).

In these early incidents, so strikingly similar in their reportage, may be found the iconography for much of the next five years' air war with Germany. The Spitfire and Hurricane pilots display brilliant airmanship as they pursue their bomber prey—"round him like flies around a honey pot," one civilian exclaims. The German crews begin the action in character, too, as they are thrown into battle in Junkers and Heinkel medium bombers, which an ill-considered Luftwaffe directive insisted be modified for dive-bombing at the expense of the speed, range, and armor that might have saved their lives against the swarming Spitfires and Hurricanes. On the ground, civilians refuse to be displaced from their daily lives—note how each writer is careful to keep his people within their usual roles—and can pity their attackers on a warmly human level. The surviving crewmen are similarly touched, and the kindness shown by these villagers makes them realize for the first time that as prisoners they will be treated decently.

The capstone to each incident comes shortly afterward when, in a spirit of chivalry so foreign to the hostile ideologies that have set their nations to war, the victorious pilots bring condolences to the surviving German crewmen. Flight Lieutenant (later Group Captain) George Pinkerton, the 602 Squadron pilot credited with the kill of Pohle's Junkers 88, visited the hospitalized German flier a few days later and recalls the meeting for Douglas McRoberts:

> "He didn't talk much. His face was a bit bashed where he'd hit the dashboard when he landed in the sea. I sent him some sweets, and some cigarettes. He wrote back to me." The letter, written from one airman to another, reads:
>
> Dear Flight Lieutenant Pinkerton,
>
> You have me make with your surprising present a very much gladness, especially I just learn in this days to comprehend the doleful fate of the prisoner of war. I thank you for the friendly conduct, wish you the best, and greet you. Likewise the other pilot. To old airmen comradeship.
>
> HELMUT C. W. POHLE,
> Hauptmann der Luftwaffe
> (p. 19)

Pohle's comrades who did not survive were buried with full military honors, the 602 Squadron's bagpipers playing in salute; four months later a wreath from Peter Townsend's 43 Squadron was placed before the coffins of the Heinkel's unlucky airmen. A harder duty awaited Townsend with Unteroffizier Karl Missy, the plane's gunner, who had survived:

> I entered and, walking straight up to his bed, held out my hand. Turning to me, he clasped it with both of his until it hurt. But it was the way he looked at me that I can never forget. We had no common tongue so could only communicate as the animals do, by touch, by expression, and by invisible means. As he took my hand Missy had in his eyes the look of a dying animal. If he had died I would have been his killer. He said nothing and only looked at me with a pitiful, frightened, and infinitely sad expres-

sion in which I thought I could recognize a glimmer of human gratitude. Indeed Missy felt no bitterness. He sank back on the pillows and I held out the bag of oranges and the tin of fifty Players I had brought for him. They seemed small compensation. (p. 208)

Meetings such as these complete the narrative cycle, concluding its action with a thought for ultimate meaning. From the high drama over the English and Scottish coasts, through the section leaders' cries of "Tally-Ho!" and the marksmanship of interception, to the spectacle witnessed by the people on the ground, these first aerial combats resolve themselves on the most personal levels of life and death. No abstractions here—no politics, no glory. If human intelligence has created war and its tools, and if the human spirit has fought wars with a high measure of courage, the final questions of death and survival are expressed on a purely natural level. Having left Unteroffizier Missy in the care of an exceptionally tender and devoted nurse, Townsend turns back to the battle, wondering if he has seen his own future: legless, burned, and disfigured, or perhaps being laid to rest in a foreign cemetery with pilots of the Luftwaffe saluting, as his fellow RAF officers had buried Karl Missy's crew.

Thus a war of epic proportions is in fact remembered by its participants as a uniquely personal affair. Although the magnificent victory roll of the Spitfire above a sunny Kentish airfield might be its public image, it is the truth of the solitary wounded airman, visited by his attacker in a dark and quiet hospital ward, that so often ends the story as a reminder of war's final reality. This tension between the physical and the spiritual characterizes the nature of the quest, from the Battle of Britain and the night fighter operations to the great offensive of Bomber Command. Here the noblest ideals of national purpose, as expressed by the greatest orators of modern times, find consequence in the struggles of individual aircrews who often face each other in single combat and pay tribute to each other's life or death. Few war stories have such commanding range, from Churchill in the House of Commons or Hitler at the Berlin Sportpalast, to Karl Missy clutching Peter Townsend's hand in Whitby Hospital.

The story demands this scope because of the special implications Great Britain and Germany faced as they went to war in 1939. In terms of relative air power, the conflict was anticipated in planning and debate for most of the previous decade. The RAF was struggling for existence within an antimilitarist government, while the Luftwaffe was being nurtured in secret as an illegal force only to be revealed, with intimidating effect, during the occupation of the Rhineland in 1936 and used as an element of bluff in subsequent Nazi advances through 1938. To many Germans, this proud new air force was an expression of national pride and power after the humiliation by the Treaty of Versailles. When the time came to rebuild the RAF, British advocates spoke in similarly epic terms, as when in 1935 the foreign secretary, Sir John Simon, advised the prime minister, "The conclusion which might have to be drawn from the above figures [of relative strength], if they are correct, is that this country is seriously open to the threat of serious attack by a continental power in a degree to which it has not been exposed for hundreds of years." The new region of vulnerability was the air, and other spokesmen were quick to cite the precedents of the Norman Invasion of 1066 and the defeat of the Spanish Armada in 1588. Such references were more than rhetorical, for the Luftwaffe's power had effectively negated Britain's island security. But this new sense of challenge set the spirit for the times, as both countries' leaders spoke of "thousand-year" consequences—the projected length of Hitler's Reich and of anticipated memory in Churchill's testament to "their finest hour." The quest was certainly one of great historical magnitude, which the key players recognized and relished—witness Hitler's fascination with Frederick the Great, and Air Chief Marshal Harris's habit of coming away from meetings with Churchill humming "Malbrouck s'en va-t-en guerre."

How did the individual airmen, both British and German, face this broadly advertised quest? They take great care in their memoirs to accommodate the long view, acknowledging their hours in the air and minutes of firing in anger (the average machine gun and cannon burst from a fighter was two seconds) as an important contribution to the measure of decades and even centuries. When in *Lions Rampant* Douglas McRoberts tells the story of the 602 City of Glasgow Squadron, he is careful to begin its narrative with the creation of the Auxiliary Air Force in 1924, Lord Trenchard's apt device for making the fighting force acceptable to a peacetime government. As the story proceeds, such exploits as flying over Mount Everest and being among the first prewar units to receive Spitfires are given detailed attention. These two benchmarks of history—one political, the other technological—are important factors in the equation that creates the Battle of Britain force. Peter Townsend enfolds his own Battle of Britain memoir within the larger sweep of history, devoting over two-thirds of *Duel of Eagles* to the development of the British and German air forces since World War I, even though the fighting of 1940 is foremost in his mind—witness his beginning with the February 3, 1940, attack on a Heinkel 111 bomber, which shaped his understanding of the war and the individuals who fought it from the air. Air Chief Marshal Sir Arthur Harris, one of the few RAF commanders to emerge from the war with issues yet to be settled (principally the morality of the indiscriminate bombing of civilians and Great Britain's appreciation of its role), sees fit to range his own story from the antizeppelin defenses in World War I and early RAF experiences in the Middle East. (Commentators have noted that such experiences as the Iraq occupation, secured by "air control" in 1922, fostered the development of an officer cadre within the air service and a tradition of a self-contained and independently directed air arm.) Harris's view is certainly among the longest, for he concludes *Bomber Offensive* with a caveat that "My part in the next war will be to be destroyed by it" (p. 280), justified by his belief that the nuclear-armed, unmanned missile will be the logical extension of the bombing attack he helped envision and execute. Harris writes from 1947, and his words have proven prophetic; what is noteworthy is that he grounds his belief in the strategy and tactics of the 1939–45 air war, whose ramifications not only have helped determine the course of world politics in the last half-century but were apparent to these airmen themselves.

From the top down the commencement of the air war between Great Britain and Germany was viewed as a monumental engagement—perhaps greater in its range of symbol, myth, and rhetoric than in military substance. But what is lost in strategic value is regained in the quality of these battles as written events, for symbol, myth, and rhetoric—and above all the conflict's iconography as it is styled in visual and verbal images—are the stuff of literature, and the writing produced from this air war is among history's best. It was also instrumental in deciding the war's outcome, for what fighters and bombers could not achieve in terms of military victory, stories about them accomplished in rhetorical effect, as world opinion was swayed and the appreciation of the war's progress was strongly enhanced.

Consider the image of the leaders. Göring, a major figure in the German government for seven years and a principal Nazi leader for nearly a decade before that, was in 1940 at the zenith of his power. Under his direction the Luftwaffe had been born and nurtured secretly, tested in Spain during the civil war, and used as an amazingly successful instrument of bluff through the political crises of 1936–38. World War II itself began with the image of his Stuka dive-bombers cutting the Polish defenses to ribbons, and seven months later his airmen quickly won mastery of the skies over France and the Low Countries, making German control of the Continent a certainty. England alone remained a hostile presence, worrisome to Hitler as a potential doorstep for reentering Western Europe. He expected the undeterred growth of German air power to frighten the British into an early armistice, and for the first eleven months of the war he forbade his bombers from attacking civilian targets for fear of stirring British popular sentiment against making peace. When the island nation continued to resist, he turned to his military leaders for help, at which point Göring grandly stepped in with the boastful offer, "Leave it to my Luftwaffe!" His last such gesture, at Dunkirk, had proved a fiasco, but earlier successes insured that some credibility in his generalship remained. The last of it would be spent in the Battle of Britain.

As a phrase, "the Battle of Britain" was coined not by a fighter or a strategist but by a statesman speaking for political effect. And what an effective speech it was, admitting that the Battle of France was over and what would be the Battle of Britain was about to begin—a struggle that for the next thousand years would be recalled as "their finest hour." *Their Finest Hour* is the title of Churchill's war-history volume devoted to the events of 1940, the theme of which he states in no uncertain terms: "How the British people held the fort ALONE till those who hitherto had been half blind were half ready." If this sentence sounds more petulant than the ringing phrases of Churchill's speeches in the House of Commons and on radio to his people and the world, it is understandable in terms of his political situation. In May 1940 he had just become prime minister of a country in contest with Germany since 1933 and at war for over half a year, for the whole time of which no single British victory had been scored, symbolic or real. Not yet a hero of the English people, he cut just the opposite figure as Göring, who had presided over success after success and was preparing to take his last grand step, right onto Churchill's unwelcome doormat. But whereas Hitler and Göring saw England as just a nuisance, for which the most offhanded planning and improvised tactics would suffice, their antagonist viewed the conflict quite differently. And it is in the difference of his formulation that the Battle of Britain's rhetorical importance can be found. "Hitler knows that he will have to break us in this island or lose the War," Churchill announced in the words following his "Battle of Britain" salutation and just before his rousing peroration anticipating "their finest hour."

On June 18, 1940, years before any military strategist could plot such a development, the prime minister revised his rhetorical theorem and thereby put himself and Britain on the offensive, even as they fought for their lives: "If we can stand up to him, all Europe may be free and the life of the world may move forward into broad uplit uplands. But if we fail, then the whole world, including the United States, including all that we have known and cared for, will sink into the abyss of a new Dark Age made more sinister, and perhaps more protracted, by the lights of perverted science."

Together, Göring's lusty boast and Churchill's apocalyptic rhetoric set the stage for the coming air war, both in the way it would be fought and, more importantly for the course of history, the way it would be written. The German image was more consistently developed and more coherent initially, for while British airmen were at play among the leisurely pursuits of university flying clubs and weekend Auxiliary Air Force duties, young Luftwaffe fliers were hard at work in an entirely new, lavishly funded and equipped arm of the service and were growing into a self-conscious elite after the humiliation of Versailles and a decade of economic stagnation. With German pride at a nadir and with little hope for gainful employment, a young man such as Franz von Werra, whose escapes from British and Canadian prisoner-of-war confinement were celebrated in Kendall Burt and James Leasor's *The One That Got Away,* found that the Luftwaffe provided all the pretentions of nobility and success the Weimar years lacked. If there was ever a "growth market," an air force career in Germany was it. The Versailles treaty after World War I had left the country with only 140 aircraft and 169 aircraft engines, all limited to strictly commercial use. Within the year gliding clubs had filled the gap, and by 1922 a secret provision of the Treaty of Rapallo had arranged for German air training in Russia in exchange for staff training of Soviet officers. In 1926 the Paris Agreement lifted the limits on civil aviation, and from then on any number of fighters and bombers could be designed, built, tested, and produced as "fast mail carriers" and "airliners."

When the Luftwaffe was unveiled on March 1, 1935, it was a creation designed to delight the eyes of German youth born into the degradation of military defeat and impoverished by economic collapse, much as National Socialism itself was packaged so attractively to appeal to a depressed German public. The first words of Heinz Knoke's *I Flew for the Führer* invoke the Pied Piper of Hamelin, who led the town's children up the road to Koppenberg, never to return. "My early years were spent on that road," Knoke confides, unwilling to say more but trustful that his metaphor will clarify the rest. For others the Luftwaffe promised rapid advancement, and its engagement in Spain allowed young men like Adolf Galland and Werner Mölders to gain both the combat experience needed for promotion and the experience in devising new tactics demanded by high-speed fighters and heavier bombers. When World War II began, there was nothing to limit these eager young men in the most handsomely endowed and Nazified of the German armed forces. With no senior officer corps above them save at the very top (where Kesselring, Sperrle, and a few others were imported from the army), the sky was quite literally the limit, and Galland and his colleagues soared high in quick successes over Poland, Norway, Holland, Belgium, and France. These victories, on the heels of the Luftwaffe's dominance in the bluffing game played in the Rhineland (where a single squadron flew from post to post in continually repainted livery), Czechoslovakia, and Austria, encouraged a high spirit dedicated to the assurance of quick and easy conquest.

In Britain, airmen felt just the opposite. In *Duel of Eagles* Peter Townsend writes of standing on alert during the Czech crisis of 1938, knowing that his squadron, in both training and equipment, was sadly unprepared for combat:

> By mid-September, shortly before the Munich Conference, we were busy getting 43 Squadron at Tangmere ready for war. We worked every night in the hangar with the ground crews, belting ammunition and (in our view an act of vandalism) daubing our silver Furies in brown and green camouflage war paint. By dawn on September 28, the day of the conference, we were ready for battle, but with what woefully inadequate weapons! A Fury [biplane] in perfect trim might reach 210 mph. The weight and friction of its war paint slowed it several mph. The modest firepower of our twin Vickers guns was academic — for the enemy bomber diagrams in the pilots' room left us all too painfully aware that we should never even catch the Heinkel 111 and Dornier 17, which did well over 250 mph.
>
> We might have found something to laugh at in the lamentable shortcomings of our equipment, but the atmosphere was too heavy with anxiety and depression for that. The older officers who had already seen one war sat around with their heads in their

hands repeating the fervent hope that they would never see another. Only [Pilot Officer] Caesar [Hull] longed to have "a crack at the Hun." (p. 152)

Townsend's fears are all the more impressive because of his training as an RAF cadet at the service college at Cranwell earlier that year. Yet the reaction of this thoroughly professional air force careerist is remarkably like that of C. F. Rawnsley, a London weekender who had joined the Auxiliary Air Force too late for pilot training and had been designated for ground service instead. By the time of the Munich Conference he had won aircrew status and passed the air gunner's test. In *Night Fighter* he recalls the panic visited upon his squadron by the suddenness of their call-up. Even with the AAF at readiness he is made to feel redundant, not because of his untempered skills but because their Demon biplanes stand no chance of even getting within range of the much faster German bombers. The crisis soon passes, and "Our time at readiness came to an end—to our relief mingled with our shame—when Neville Chamberlain returned from Munich and waved that piece of paper at the cheering crowds." This is not to say that the squadron believes the prime minister's message. "We felt that the day of reckoning had merely been postponed, and that no political claptrap about 'peace in our time' could stall off much longer the clash that was bound to occur so long as the Nazis were allowed to continue having their own way" (pp. 22–23).

So ends 1938, with two opposing air forces yet to go to war but possessing directly opposite self-images: the Luftwaffe glorying in its new state-of-the-art equipment, excellent training, and combat experience in Spain, while the RAF sits in obsolete aircraft fearing the worst. But there remained another stage of development before their face-to-face combat would begin in the Battle of Britain. In September 1939, just a year after sitting out the Munich crisis in their outdated Furies and Demons, Townsend and Rawnsley found the war beginning with their squadrons equipped with an entirely new generation of planes—the Hurricane and Blenheim respectively. The former had the speed to reach the bombers and the maneuverability to mix it with the best of the Luftwaffe's fighters; the Blenheim gave a back-seat man like Rawnsley a new weapon, radar, by which to engage the enemy. For the next nine months Townsend and Rawnsley would hone their skills in these new aircraft, flying cover for coastal convoys, practicing night interceptions, and engaging the odd German intruder over the North Sea or English Channel. They fired few shots in anger but developed a proficiency with their new weapons that would prove deadly to the Germans when the Battle began in earnest the following July.

By midsummer 1940, when the Luftwaffe was flying thousands of sorties per day over southeast England, the character of the air war had changed radically. In the Rhineland and during the Czech and Austrian crises their weaponry had been simply bluff, and as the war began in Poland the shots they fired were for the most part at aircraft on the ground—much of the Polish Air Force was destroyed before it could take off. Seven months later the air forces of France, Belgium, and Holland failed to offer formidable resistance; it was considered remarkable at the time that Condor Legion ace Werner Mölders should be downed by a French fighter. But by July 1940 Luftwaffe pilots—aces and otherwise—were falling by the score, and aircraft dumps of wrecked Messerschmitts, Stukas, Heinkels, Junkers, and Dorniers littered the English countryside, as for the first time in its history Göring's elite service was being relentlessly challenged in the air.

Adolf Galland notes in *The First and the Last* that his pilots were being challenged on the ground as well. After a month of service on the Channel he recalls reporting back to Berlin and being dismayed at the capital's picture of "peaceful serenity" where the war "had hardly made any difference to the daily life at home." Cinemas and theaters were crowded, and shops did good business with the well-paid populace, which had not yet been called up for service. Even the outer husk of German life remained untouched by the war Galland had just been fighting, on increasingly dangerous terms:

> Was one to take this as a bad or a good omen? The I-could-not-care-less attitude at home and the general lack of interest in the war did not please me. I had come straight out of a battle for life and death, the brunt of which so far had been borne by the fighter force. Naturally we had no insight into the ramifications of this war, but we guessed fairly accurately that the battle we were fighting on the Channel was of decisive importance to the continuance and the final outcome of the struggle. (pp. 33–34).

Above all, Galland is aware of a vexing new problem in the Luftwaffe's air war—the RAF's determined resistance—and to illustrate it he devises the perfect simile:

> We were aware that it needed a tremendous concentration of strength in order to emerge victoriously, and we felt that our own strength was being overtaxed. The colossus of World War II seemed to be like a pyramid turned upside down, balancing on its apex, not knowing which way to lean. And for a moment the whole burden of the war rested on the few hundred German fighter pilots on the Channel coast. (p. 34)

Thus, the concept of "the few" becomes a motivating force not just for RAF strategy, but in the German view as well.

When the few in Britain face off against the few from Germany, it is the RAF that wins the battle, whose small number of combatants guarantees that its outcome will be of principally symbolic consequence. Because of this emphasis on symbolism and iconography, the numerical inferiority of the British forces gives them an advantage over the better-manned and better-equipped aggressor. For the Battle of Britain Göring could launch a thousand bombers and two hundred fifty dive-bombers, escorted by well over a thousand fighters. Against these numbers Dowding and his group commanders could count on just 331 Hurricanes and Spitfires after the Dunkirk evacuation. By mid July the total of single-engine, operational frontline fighters had risen to 531, but once the Battle began RAF pilots would perish at the rate of 300 per month, with only 260 replacements expected — inexperienced men, often with less than ten hours on Spitfires or Hurricanes, doomed to become pitiably quick casualties. Whether in terms of the initial face-off or attrition, Fighter Command was engaged in a losing contest, a situation seen most dramatically in the task faced by Keith Park in command of 11 Group, which had only sixteen squadrons (less than 192 operational fighters) to defend London and all of southeast England from Norwich to Southampton through seventeen hours of light each day.

To fight such long odds, certain tactics had to be improvised. Weather delays were especially fortuitous, as when during a five-day interruption of Luftwaffe attacks Fighter Command was able to receive fifty new pilots without suffering combat losses. But loss rates were such that by mid August Park had to order his pilots to engage the enemy only over land or within gliding distance of the coast. "During the next two or three weeks," he cautioned, "we cannot afford to lose pilots through forced landings in the sea." Moreover, their role was to be exclusively defensive, to protect sector airfields rather than engage in free-lance combat with German fighters, a style of warfare Göring was trying to provoke. A third plan led to one of the greatest military controversies of the war, as Park's request for airfield defense from neighboring 12 Group to the north was frustrated by Trafford Leigh-Mallory's tactic of forming three or more squadrons into "big wings," the better to attack, scatter, and decimate Luftwaffe bomber fleets (often on their way home), but at a crucial cost in time—only single squadrons could scramble quickly enough to defend the southern group's airfields before attack. Even at this high level of command decision individual pilots were involved—some backing Park, others, such as Douglas Bader, taking matters into their own hands in the air and arguing their case directly to the Air Staff on the ground. But underlying these improvisations was a structure whose design frustrated the generally unplanned German strategy of assault by weight of numbers: sector control. Each RAF group was subdivided into several smaller sectors, where ground controllers would receive general orders from group command and interpret them according to the local strength available. That the Germans did not understand this structure or consider it important is shown by their disinterest in keeping early-warning radar, the eyes of this system, out of commission and by their failure to distinguish sector control airfields—where British operations rooms were especially vulnerable to attack—from other fighter bases.

Improvisation within a sound, well-planned system remains the key to RAF success, with a corresponding failure on the German side that to Adolf Galland becomes even more clear in retrospect:

> Again it was the fault of the over-all strategical concept in our conduct of the war that made the task of the Luftwaffe and in particular that of our fighters so difficult and exhausting. In the summer of 1940 we had quickly and unexpectedly come into possession of the west European Atlantic coast, a position which imperatively made England the strategic target. In the summer of 1942 we stood equally unexpectedly on the Egyptian border, from where it suddenly seemed possible to cut one of the essential British lifelines. In both cases we hoped to achieve our goal with insufficient forces and with quick improvisation. Both attempts were just as unsuccessful. (pp. 146–47)

Not only was insufficient thought given to the air war with England, but an overall view was lacking as well. Whereas the three massive German air fleets, or Luftflotten, functioned separately—

sometimes at odds with each other and with Göring's erratic commands—RAF Fighter Control kept the situation most capably in hand, as Allen Andrews appreciates in *The Air Marshals:*

> It was a highly intricate coordination of radar, radio-telegraphy, telephony, radio-telephony, cerebral calculation and fighting resourcefulness. Radar, radio-telegraphy and physical observation were the means of detecting the position of all airborne machines, friend or foe. The radar stations on the coast indicated enemy machines approaching Britain and their approximate force; tellers in the Royal Observer Corps reported the numbers, positions, course and estimated height of those aircraft they could see or detect acoustically; an electronic direction-indicating device in all home aircraft identified them as friend, not foe, and gave their bearing. Information from these three sources was coordinated and expressed as symbols on a huge map in an operations room, giving the complete picture of the situation in the air from moment to moment.
>
> The action essential to meet attack was ordered according to the information concerning approaching raiders. Squadrons were put into the air, and followed while in the air. A fighter controller in a subordinate [sector] operations room kept in touch with the leaders of his squadrons by radio-telephone. Dead reckoning plotters in the operations room calculated the courses necessary to set the fighters to intercept the raiders. The controller passed on these recommended courses and heights, and maintained authority until the fighters saw the enemy. During the action he followed the battle by listening out on the radio-telephone. If fresh enemy forces were detected near the battle area he would warn his fighter leaders. When the battle was over he resumed command and either directed his formation to further action or nursed them back to base. (pp. 107–8).

From Air Chief Marshal Dowding, who shared the key 11 Group control room at Uxbridge with Air Vice-Marshal Park, down through the seven sector controllers in 11 Group to the squadrons scrambled from the various airfields within each sector and the airborne pilots talking with their sector controllers, the entire Battle over London and southeast England was fought under almost perfect control—a quality the Luftwaffe forces lacked. Combined with other factors in the RAF's favor, including fighting for and above one's homeland in one's own weather, the numerical odds of the Battle of Britain were sharply reduced. But numbers were what the world saw, and when the

Spitfire and Hurricane squadrons began downing disproportionate ratios of both enemy fighters and bombers, opinion quickly shifted to proclaim a new winner in the war.

That the claims were inflated, a result of honest confusion in the heat of combat and the Air Ministry's decision to let them stand as obvious morale boosters, does not diminish the fact that the skies over England saw some of the bravest and most spectacular fighting of the war. German pilots felt less political animosity toward their RAF foes than toward the general situation, which compelled them to secure their Western Wall so that they could turn to the extinction of what was perceived to be both Germany's and the West's historic foe, Russian Bolshevism; few Luftwaffe memoirists, whether commanders or flying noncoms, fail to mention this fact. But in their defensive role, especially as played at odds against a savage intruder, the RAF writers had a deeper history to draw upon, and C. F. Rawnsley is quick to make the historical comparison when his night fighter squadron is posted to Middle Wallop in Wiltshire, set among the Iron Age hill forts and tenements of Britain's past: "It was a comforting thought that here, under the shadow of the grass-covered stronghold of Danebury Hill, the descendants of those ancient Britons were toiling like beavers to raise a new rampart against the invaders" (p. 33).

With the Luftwaffe flying from captured bases in France, while the RAF fights in both friendlier and more appropriately historical environs, the talents for metaphor-making are more convincingly allied with Rawnsley and his comrades. It is the Spitfire's engine that was given the richly evocative name Merlin; a long line of Hawker fighters bears names that reflect Britain's island nature: Hurricane, Tempest, and (with a bow to the far-flung regions of its empire) Typhoon. Auxiliary Air Force units, now fully integrated with the RAF and drawing new personnel from the same training pool, nevertheless retain their badges and names: City of Glasgow Squadron, City of London Squadron. Enhancing this sense of spirited local defense is the Spitfire Fund, through which aircraft are endowed by towns, industries, and other private concerns, to the point of bearing their legends beneath the cockpits. The pilots are equally devoted, sleeping beneath the Hurricane and Spitfire wings or even at the controls, ready to be airborne in less than two minutes.

There is an occasional touch of humor — sometimes slapstick, sometimes grim — to the whole affair. In order to learn the procedures of radiotelephony all the more graphically pilots are taken to a football stadium in Uxbridge, where they mount Walls' ice-cream tricycles and are ordered about the field by their controller to simulate flight operations. At Hawkinge, an RAF field within sight of the Pas de Calais from which the German air fleets set out, a fighter lands to refuel with holes in its propeller, only to have them caulked solid with an aircraftman's chewing gum. On the grim side, RAF pilots burned to death in their crashed fighters are often identified in the local press as Poles or Czechs to make the news easier for the populace to accept. A leading ace, Flight Commander A. G. "Sailor" Malan, boasts to his mates that he prefers to damage rather than down enemy bombers so that they arrive back at base with the dead and dying as a blow to Luftwaffe morale. Both Douglas Bader (as quoted in *Reach for the Sky*) and the pilots of 602 Squadron (as reported in *Lions Rampant*) claim credit for downing enemy aircraft without firing a shot, by intimidating them through circling maneuvers until the enemy plane turns for home ("one aircraft badly frightened") or is driven into the ground ("one aircraft frightened to death"). Luftwaffe pilots are doubly victimized when, in good humor, they are asked to contribute to the neighborhood's Spitfire Fund after crashing in London's East End.

There is even a comic sense to operations themselves, as radar operator C. F. Rawnsley, peering down the dim fuselage of his Beaufighter, remarks to pilot John Cunningham how much the scene resembles the London Underground:

> To complete the illusion, I switched on a few shaded lights along the cat-walk between the cannon. The little pools of yellow light shining along the metal hull, the rattling on the roof, and the blue flickering and flashing light all added up to just the right effect.
>
> "Leicester Square . . . change for the Piccadilly Line," I started chanting. "Mind the doors . . . ri-i-ght!" (p. 191)

Rawnsley has an eye for light, just as another memoirist, Pierre Closterman of the Free French RAF "Alsace" Squadron, is sensitive to the colors of the German planes he encounters. As always, the metaphors come from home — here football and the pyrotechnics of Guy Fawkes Day — as Rawnsley describes Luftwaffe navigation:

> To help their planes find their way back the Germans projected two searchlight beams vertically on the coast near Dunkirk. They stood like goalposts to mark the limits of play. . . .

At the other end of the field, when the raiders headed toward London, our home goal was clearly marked once the show had started by a highly impressive display of shell bursts, tracer and rocket showers which we referred to somewhat disparagingly as "Pile's Fireworks," named after the Commander-in-Chief of Anti-Aircraft Command. (p. 249)

A more specific sense of hilarity invades Group Captain J. E. "Johnnie" Johnson's *Wing Leader,* when much later in the war, as his squadron occupies a forward airfield in Normandy, a Spitfire is designated for catering service to fly in victuals from a home-base restauranteer and is fitted with a barrel of beer on its bomb rack. Few pages of any RAF operations memoir can pass without at least one such comic episode, whereas the Luftwaffe accounts of this stage of the fighting are generally without humor, save that expressed in ironic exasperation with its leadership.

Yet even in the RAF narratives with their happy-go-lucky moments, it is the serious side of battle that gets most of the attention. The fledgling night fighter squadrons feel it the most, for with their still rudimentary equipment they are virtually powerless to repulse the most humanly catastrophic of the Luftwaffe's onslaught: the bombing of London, whose flames of devastation mock their efforts each night. As opposed to the Spitfire squadrons engaged in dogfights at twenty thousand feet and more, well in advance of the daytime targets, Peter Townsend's and C. F. Rawnsley's units fly at a lower altitude within sight of a burning London. From his vantage point on patrol Townsend complains that "It was tormenting, in all that immensity of black sky, to look down on London three miles beneath me, consumed by fire and torn by the blast of bombs and landmines whose fiery conflagrations rent the darkness below." In his solitary Hurricane, lacking radar and as yet only improvising tactics with ground control, his report is bleakly demoralizing: "For two hours, while the enemy was killing hundreds of our people, I searched in vain, desperate and ashamed at our impotence to defend the defenseless" (*Duel in the Dark,* p. 134). But here again the long tradition of history enhances Townsend's perspective and aids his resolve, for the Great City Fire of December 29 (when a low tide leaves little water in the Thames to douse the flames) reminds the pilot not just of "a huge brazier" but of the fact that "Nothing like it had been seen since the Great Fire of 1666, when the diarist John Evelyn wrote that he witnessed 'a blood red sky, painted by a myriad of seething fires' " (p.

141). Townsend's own text is thus linked to history, promising an equally historic and therefore inevitable recovery, for when he realizes that a countryman three centuries before faced the same task of recording London's destruction by flames, all need not be lost. This is the night, however, when the most of London's cherished architecture burns: the Guildhall, County Hall, and eight Wren churches. The task of postwar rebuilding would be akin to that of 1666, at least in sentiment.

C. F. Rawnsley sees much the same from the back seat of his Blenheim, but he feels even worse when witnessing the sight from London itself when home on leave. "I looked up as the raider droned unscathed across the night sky," he notes, "and I began to feel sick and ashamed that we should apparently be doing so little about stopping this bombing. And I was ashamed and angry with myself for not being back with the squadron, and at least trying to get at those raiders" (p. 64). Back at Middle Wallop with 604 Squadron, however, he feels equally powerless each time a Junkers or Dornier eludes his interception, which with faulty electronic equipment happens almost every time. He is obsessed with the fear of failing at his job and tormented by his inability to turn matters around: "I became more and more conscious of the thought that every incoming raider that evaded us carried a bomb that might kill a lot of people, even a dozen mothers, and it began to prey upon my conscience" (p. 297). These worries grow to form a subtext in Rawnsley's *Night Fighter,* leading to that type of combat fatigue known as "the twitch" and causing him to lose for a time his sense of confidence, even though as teamed with pilot John Cunningham he forms one of the best night fighting crews of the war. Such are the wages of fighting above a London in flames.

A day fighter pilot can share this dismay, but in *Wing Leader* Johnnie Johnson expresses the dilemma in figures rather than in the images that, experienced first hand, so wrenched Rawnsley's conscience. Even after the Luftwaffe is driven from the daytime skies, its bombers remain active at night, ranging as far as cities in the West and Midlands:

> The dreadful inadequacy of our night defenses at this time can well be imagined from the stark fact that for every 1000 bombers that crossed our coasts only six were brought down by ack-ack or night fighters. For instance, on 14th November 1940, when Coventry was attacked by more than 300 bombers, only one Blenheim was able to open fire against the invaders. Later in the

month, when Birmingham and Liverpool were fiercely attacked
at night, not a single bomber was intercepted. (p. 56)

From the German side, Junkers 88 pilot Peter Stahl logs fifty missions over England before encountering a single night fighter, and
even then the moonlight is such that he can easily avoid his enemy.
Yet for the memoirist there is the sense that this battle is unfolding as much like drama as history, and Rawnsley is quick to rise from
his malaise to take pleasure in a self-consciously unfolding scene.
Again it is the peculiar nature of British government, history, and
culture that sets the stage, particularly when it comes time for the
nation's leader to visit the front. In Germany the prospect is less
appealing, whether it be Hitler fuming in Berlin or Göring, in his
lavishly equipped personal train, steaming into the Pas de Calais to
seize a radio reporter's microphone and impetuously announce his
own generalship of the air battle. The Nazis' roots, after all, reach
back only to 1933, and their Thousand-Year Reich is still in its first
decade. But when Rawnsley's squadron stands for review, the
honored guest is His Royal Majesty King George VI, stately and
reserved, universally loved by his countrymen since regretfully assuming the monarchy in 1936 and in the process maintaining a kingship
dating back to Arthur. Rawnsley starts with a bit of fun, noting the
King's enquiry as to why the radar operators do not wear flying
badges and then being able to give King George his own score and the
promise that yes, at the Sovereign's request, he will "get another one
to-night" (p. 130). How different would be the tone of such a scene
between Göring and a Luftwaffe airman, and how short of the fairy-
tale ending that happens when later that night a Heinkel comes over
and is intercepted and downed by none other than Cunningham and
Rawnsley. "We got back to base shortly after midnight," Rawnsley
writes, "and John immediately had an enthusiastic call from Brownie
[their commander]. He reported that His Majesty and the C.-in-C.
had heard the combat, and that they had seen the burning Heinkel fall
from the sky. No showman could have wished for better timing or a
better setting" (pp. 133–34). A "Command Performance" indeed, as
Rawnsley puts it, and once again an event whose terms would have
played so differently among the German forces, whose use of this
phrase more often implies the Gestapo.
A certain amount of fear leads to dishonorable conduct, which
mars the RAF chronicle. The station at Manston was especially
vulnerable to both bombings and fighter strafings, and its exposed

setting atop a cliff alongside the sea was not conducive to good groundcrew morale. After an especially severe Luftwaffe attack on August 12 many aircraftmen resolved to spend their entire days within the air-raid shelters and did not even come out to collect their pay. A similar situation lasted for weeks at Middle Wallop among the crews servicing day fighters. In the air all was not courage and glamor; while some deaths were heroic, others were not, as Johnnie Johnson confides in *Wing Leader:*

> From our cockpits we watched a burning Spitfire. We could do nothing except wait for the parachute to flare out and then pass an accurate fix to Tangmere for the rescue operation. But instead of using these few precious seconds to bale out the man inside suddenly panicked and screamed over the radio. We had never heard this sort of thing before, and for a few shocked moments we listened to his dreadful mouthings. We were a lot of dirty bastards! It was our fault he was on fire! He was going to die! Alone. We would leave him. And not return. We . . .
>
> I came out of my stupor and flicked on my transmitter switch to jam this creature's accusations. Mercifully the radio was silent and we watched the Spitfire smack into the cold sea at a shallow angle. I passed a fix to Tangmere and flew low over the sea. The heaving waters had already closed in and there was no sign of wreckage or dinghy. The seven of us flew back to Tangmere together, and did not speak again until we were on the ground. (pp. 134–35)

The fact is that despite the presence of his wingmen and squadron mates, Johnson's pilot is quite alone, sealed beyond reach in the cockpit of a burning machine hurtling through space at several hundred miles per hour over an unwelcoming sea. Another Spitfire pilot, Pierre Closterman, comments on the special nature of the warfare these fliers undertake—so different from the bayonet charge, for example, where the dangers of combat are shared by "a thousand human beings, sweating with fear, supporting and sustaining each other in a helpless, anonymous massacre." In the air it is just the opposite. "For us, it was a deliberate, individual act, a conscious, scientific sacrifice. Unaided, alone, each one of us had every day to conquer the stab of fear in our breast, to preserve, re-form, our ebbing store of will power" (p. 147), and then after every mission reassume the practice of a normal life. A combat sortie is itself a roller coaster of emotions; for Johnson the giddy peak comes at the moment of identifying his foe: "Recognition came and with it the usual shocked heart-in-mouth feeling which was always the same — exactly the sort of sensation you get when your car slides out of control on a greasy road" (p. 240).

There are tactics for avoiding this fear. Hearing the masterful voice of your squadron leader is one of the best, and Douglas Bader cultivated the technique of speaking confidently to his pilots at key points throughout their attacks, combining wit and personality with the deep knowledge of an experienced fighter ace. Bader's story also shows an amazing style of aggressiveness not only in aerial combat but in skirmishes with commanders over his belief in big-wing attacks and more active free-lance fighter sweeps. After one period of especially vexing inactivity he telephones Group Commander Trafford Leigh-Mallory late at night to complain that their guns are rusting up. Bader also acts with fierce independence by rejecting the new canon-equipped Spitfire VBs in favor of his older Mark II with machine guns, arguing that the new, heavier armament reduced maneuverability and encouraged pilots to stay at too wide a range.

Such eager aggression far outweighs timidity in these fighter pilots' memoirs. As squadron leaders, Bader and Johnson are forever anxious to keep their units in action; even when Dowding's rotation scheme takes them to 13 Group in Scotland for a time, the pilots are promised that soon their leader will "get them back to the South" where the war is being fought. As Bader phones Leigh-Mallory, Johnson travels directly to Fighter Command Headquarters at Bentley Priory to implore Air Chief Marshal Sholto Douglas to put his squadron back in the action before their skills are blunted and their spirits fade. Later, at Wittering, Johnson's station commander is Basil Embry, the group captain who, after being shot down over France, killed his prison guards, escaped to Spain, and returned to flying under an assumed name because the Germans had ordered his execution if captured again. His wing leader, Pat Jameson, had escaped the Norway debacle in 1940 by landing his Hurricane on the aircraft carrier *Glorious,* only to survive again that ship's sinking. Another younger pilot loses an eye in combat but wins his fight to stay on flying duty. Such was the quality of men with whom Johnson served.

Exploits such as these foster the fighter-leader mystique, which receives its greatest play in Paul Brickhill's account of Douglas Bader's life, *Reach for the Sky* (which was made into a successful film in the mid 1950s period when RAF glamor was at its height). "I think he almost eliminated fear from his pilots," Air Vice-Marshal Tom Pike attests to Brickhill, an RAF crewman famous for participating in and writing *The Great Escape.* "His semi-humorous, bloodthirsty outlook was exactly what is wanted in war and their morale soared. He was a tremendous tonic" (p. 273). But the Bader myth runs much deeper, as it must to have motivated so many men in the war and to have fascinated even more readers and filmgoers in the decades afterward. He behaves like a dynamo because he is forever "proving himself" (p. 197), a compulsion stirred by the "entrenched demon" within him, which had prodded him to excel at school sports as a small boy and to make a gallant career in the wartime RAF as a legless pilot. For such a man there is no past or future, just the "agreeable present" (p. 24), within which he can function freely—a prescription written to order for air combat in a Spitfire or Hurricane. From his peacetime injury (due to inexcusable recklessness in forbidden low-altitude aerobatics) through his wartime adventures (which included the charming of his Luftwaffe captors), Bader is the ikon of the wounded pilot, the fallen knight, as first recognized by the nurses who treat the double-amputee:

> It had become a personal fight with her and other nurses to save the young man's life. Usually they were impartial and impersonal about patients, but this one was somehow different. He seemed too young and too handsome to die, and everyone kept asking about him. On the second morning she was turning the limp body with the help of another nurse when he suddenly sat up and kissed her, then sank back into unconsciousness again. She was petrified with amazement. "Not so unconscious after all," observed the other nurse slyly. Thornhill lifted his eyelid back with a gentle thumb but he *was* unconscious. (p. 56)

No matter what his condition, Bader never stops fighting. He declines the Luftwaffe's chivalrous offer of free passage for a British plane to bring a replacement for his damaged artificial leg, preferring that a Blenheim drop it on a normal bombing raid. As the war ends three and a half years later, he tries to borrow a Spitfire for one last sortie, and even when this ploy fails he cannot resist regretting that the fight is over.

Why are men such as Bader revered as heroes, when there is so much bravado in their conduct that in normal times they might be condemned as irresponsible renegades? Pierre Closterman hints at an answer in the beginning of *The Big Show,* as he measures what the war will demand of him:

> I felt very nervous. I was curious, and anxious at the same time, to know how I would react in the face of danger, a rather morbid wish to know what fear felt like—real fear, the fear of man, alone, face to face with death. And yet there remains, deeply rooted, the old scepticism of the civilized human being; the routine of work, travel in comfort, the humanities, city life—all this, in truth, leaves very little room for a realization of mortal danger or for any testing of purely physical courage. (p. 21)

The peculiar nature of the air war that began in 1940 provided just such tests and just such promises of an answer. Here would be no comforting routine of daily life, for thousands of German aircraft were massed against a scant five hundred or so defenders. But neither would the action be abstract and anonymous as much of the Great War's fighting had been, for now a single man could lead his Spitfire against a single, visible enemy, each relying on personally honed skills to decide the contest—with the foe, with his own courage and nerve. For swashbucklers such as Bader and sensitive observers such as Closterman the field is open both to act and to write. Even an unidealistic young man such as Richard Hillary, who begins the war as an Oxford student in the mold of those carefree, cynical hedonists of Evelyn Waugh novels, can be aware of the special scope offered by the coming conflict. Knowing that war is inevitable, he is depressed by the politicians' failure and his own consequently needless risk. "We hoped merely that when war came it might be fought with a maximum of individuality and a minimum of discipline" (p. 14), he recalls, anticipating just the style that would prove so suitable an ikon for Bader. True, Hillary's generation is called disillusioned and spoiled, superficially "selfish and egocentric without any Holy Grail in which we could lose ourselves" (p. 27), but the heroic aspects of the coming battle more than overcome these deficiencies, in terms more positive than Closterman's test of civilization:

> I say that I am fighting this war because I believe that, in war, one can swiftly develop all one's faculties to a degree it would normally take half a lifetime to achieve. And to do this you must be as free from outside interference as possible. That's why I'm in the Air Force. For in a Spitfire we're back to war as it ought to be—if you can talk about war as it ought to be. Back to individual combat, to self-reliance, total responsibility for one's own fate. One either kills or is killed; and it's damned exciting. (p. 90)

Hillary foresees a swift and clean engagement with an equally swift and clean resolution: "It's exciting, it's individual, and it's disinterested. I shan't be sitting behind a long-range gun working out how to kill people sixty miles away. I shan't get maimed: either I shall get killed or I shall get a few pleasant putty medals and enjoy being stared at in a night club" (p. 17). Irony provides that Hillary does get maimed, and horribly; over half of *The Last Enemy* chronicles his arduously painful recovery from burns and reconstructive surgery, and even though he returns to service, a flying accident ends his life before the war is half-through. The hospital ward, where Peter Townsend spent those heart-wrenching minutes with his victim, Karl Missy, is the reverse side of the coin stamped by the qualities of man-to-man warfare. Except in the classic scene of generals meeting in victory and surrender, foes rarely share so close a presence, whether in combat or its aftermath.

Thus reads the battle's anticipation and conclusion. Within it lies another feature, one touched on time and again in the finest passages of war memoirs—the joy of flight. For Pierre Closterman it is ample compensation for all the risk and fear, because flight provides a wealth of sensation for both living and writing:

> When I took off by the light of the flare path and began to climb on my course it was still pitch dark. I could dimly see the vague phosphorescences of my instruments and the blue flames, punctuated by red sparks, vomited by my exhaust.
>
> I climbed hard and fast and crossed the English coast at about 22,000 feet. The fog was concentrated in the narrow valleys in long milky trails. The atmosphere was so calm that I could distinguish in the shadows, over there in the distance, the smoke of a train near Dungeness, motionless, as if anchored to the ground. The Channel was but an indistinct opaque mass with a vague silver hem along the cliffs. Not a cloud anywhere.
>
> I climbed through the darkness embracing the earth towards the now luminous sky and the dimming stars.
>
> Suddenly, without any transition, I plunged like a diver into full golden light. The wings of my Spitfire turned crimson. I was so dazzled that I had to lower my smoked glasses over my eyes. Beyond Holland, far away over there on the left, the sun emerged like a molten ingot from the inert leaden mass of the North Sea.
>
> Beneath my wings was night—I was alone, 30,000 feet up in the daylight. I was the first to breathe in the warm life of the

sun's rays, which pierce the eyeballs like arrows. In France, in England, in Belgium, in Holland, in Germany, men were suffering in the night, whilst I, alone in the sky, was the sole possessor of the dawning day—all was mine, the light, the sun; and I thought with calm pride: all this is shining only for me! (*The Big Show,* p. 45)

Positioned as God, Closterman reacts as a poet, as do many other airmen, including C. F. Rawnsley:

And then it began to get light above us, and suddenly, like a submarine surfacing, we broke through the cloud and into a fantastic wonderland floodlit with purple light. The whole western sky was still ablaze with the glory of the afterglow. We were heading into it, and behind us the first faint stars were beginning to peep out. Below us the cloud swept to the horizon in a smooth carpet of purple snow, and in all that world we were the only living things: no reconnaissance aircraft, no firelighters, not even Father Christmas with his sleigh. (*Night Fighter,* pp. 77–78)

Purple snow, crimson wings, all in a solitary world suspended above the earthbound night below—a wonder of natural beauty, as one sight after another dazzles the beholder. Later in the war, on a high-altitude interception, Rawnsley notices the curvature of the earth, a breathtaking view that anticipates the rapturous accounts of the first astronauts a quarter century later.

Yet human life is an earthly affair, and after the risks of flight Closterman is quick to attest to "The usual sensation of being born all over again at the moment when your tyres screech on the concrete" (p. 202). And there is certainly an earthly mission to fulfill, a fight to fight, which if lost will, in words first distrusted by Richard Hillary but later taken to heart in the real theme of his memoir, extinguish all courage in the world—"the courage to love, to create, to take risks, whether physical or intellectual or moral" (p. 87). Men must never hesitate to carry out the promptings of their hearts, he learns, or else emotion will atrophy.

The conclusion is success, as measured in the subtitles to the RAF's official three-volume history of the war: the fight at odds, the fight avails, the fight is won. Within this structure pilots and crews find apt expression for their stories, whether in the dazzling heights above England and Europe or in the darkness of a hospital ward where they and their enemies mend. The evidence of their quest is in their exploits; but it is also in their writing, and the best of these memoirs end with a sad leave-taking from their weapons of war.

For Pierre Closterman the moment comes on an airfield in Denmark nearly three months after his last operational sortie. There is still exhilaration in the air, as he loops and rolls his plane, the better to remember its supple, docile control. But on touching down he weeps as never before when he drops his plane to the ground "like a cut flower" (p. 216), never to hold it again.

For Douglas Bader his last time at the controls is a mixture of nostalgia and feistiness, when during the first Battle of Britain Day Flypast in 1945 he lifts his Spitfire from the runway at North Weald and heads for London. "Once, over the city, he remembered the battle and for a moment, nostalgically, wanted to fight it again" (p. 364).

3

The Personality
of Squadron Life

THE first thing one notes when opening a memoir or history of air combat in World War II is the role played by squadron life. In the First World War, individuals drew more attention than the group; aces such as Rickenbacker, Bishop, Richthofen, and Guynemer were much better known than their squadrons, which often took their names. In 1940, however, air combat assumed strategic importance, especially as it was conceived by its participants and presented to the world, with individual exploits making their contribution but never overwhelming the atmosphere of collective effort.

The most readily recalled picture of the Battle of Britain today, because it had the widest distribution as a news photo from 1940 onward, is not that of a flight of Hurricanes diving into a Luftwaffe bomber formation or of a Spitfire locked in combat with a yellow-nosed Messerschmitt but rather that of the twelve men of an RAF squadron lounging in the deck chairs and on the grass of a sunny Kentish airfield, waiting for the scramble call to take them aloft. Here one finds room for the full range of physical types and personalities: the patrician flight lieutenant, a service careerist, drawing on his pipe as he scans the *Times* in his chair; the dapper pilot officer, late of the weekenders' Auxiliary Air Force, adapting to his new life in this "finest flying club in the world" by catching some sunshine on the lawn; and the ruddy sergeant-pilot, whose service began with wartime conscription, recently arrived from an Operational Training Unit and masking his fear by frolicking with the squadron puppy. The inevitable mascot recalls Randall Jarrell's poem about a similar group of airmen, "Eighth Air Force":

If, in an odd angle of the hutment,
A puppy laps the water from a can
Of flowers, and the drunk sergeant shaving
Whistles *O Paradiso!* — shall I say that man
Is not as men have said: a wolf to man?

The other murders troop in yawning;
Three of them play Pitch, one sleeps, and one
Lies counting missions, lies there sweating
Till even his heart beats: One; One; One.
O murderers! . . . Still, this is how it's done:

This is a war. But since these play, before they die,
Like puppies with their puppy; since, a man,
I did as these have done, but did not die —
I will content the people as I can
And give up these to them: Behold the man!

I have suffered, in a dream, because of him,
Many things; for this last savior, man,
I have lied as I lie now. But what is lying?
Men wash their hands, in blood, as best they can:
I find no fault in this just man.

It is squadron life, the poet sees, that humanizes the otherwise beastly slaughter. Across the Channel a German squadron will be doing much the same — perhaps enjoying a fine French wine rather than bitters or a Guinness, and sometimes indulging in mascots as exotic as lion or tiger cubs, but otherwise forming a complementary picture, where the card game is Skat instead of Pitch and the planes bear black crosses and swastikas instead of tricolored roundels. As with Jarrell's airmen, the killing will soon follow.

Given the mortal consequence of their duties, it is easy to understand why the memoirists seize upon these details of daily life within their squadrons, for here is the regimen to insulate them from the horrors of their work. No matter what their branch of air service, they have a special fondness for close description of the station and its squadron life, against whose regularity their adventures in the air are played out. Early in *Lancaster Target* Jack Currie offers an account of the airfield at Wickenby with its runway layout, but soon he is savoring the particulars of several years' life there: the flight huts and crew quarters "hid in a shallow grove of ash, birch and elm trees," the mighty bombers flashing back the sun from their perspex canopies and turrets, the growl of a Merlin engine being tested, the "petrol bowser humming towards dispersal, a tractor pulling a long train of bomb trolleys, a faded windsock flapping gently on its mast, and a crimson signature of the sun on a few lines of cirrus cloud"—all of which prompts him to stray from his strict account and indulge in sweet nostalgia and sometimes lush writing, as the flow of narrative grants him the privilege to "sit on the grass and absorb the scene" (p. 32). In *The Eighth Passenger,* bomb aimer Miles Tripp recalls the special nature of a fogged-in airfield, where "The following days had a detached, dream-like quality. A mesh of mist trailed over trees that were bare except for sprays of yellowing leaves and the sweet smell of decaying vegetation prevailed over the more familiar smells of high octane fuel and exhaust fumes. Even time seemed to hover like the mist. Sounds became muted and colours blurred in this soft null of drifting November" (p. 36). Tripp draws out the sensuous details of this scene as a prelude to the paragraph in which he falls in love.

Night fighter crews have feelings for the entirely different dimensions of their own work, and when C. F. Rawnsley prepares to leave 604 Squadron's Middle Wallop for a rest with a training unit he recalls the scene in loving detail:

> We were saying good-bye to the fine, free life that only those who have served with a squadron can know. My thoughts turned to the freshness of the dawn, and I remembered the larks getting up from under our feet, the dew dripping from shrouded aircraft as heavy-eyed fitters pulled off engine covers, the magical hush of evening as we sat outside the crew room on a warm summer night and Johan lazily tossed pebbles to fool the twisting bats. And I saw again the razor-sharp silhouette of the first patrol climbing away into the gathering dusk.
>
> I recalled the unforgettable smells: the sweet, nostalgic and quite incongruous mixture of wet grass and warm tarmac, of new mown hay and high octane petrol, and the whiff of dope thinners in the clean night air. (p. 196)

A poet with his senses, Rawnsley finds his lyric ready-made in the contrasts and synesthesias of the airfield setting animated by his squadron's presence. His next station, West Malling, is even more typical of the airfields that took center stage in the Battle of Britain three years before: deep in the heart of Kentish hop country, it is set in a

region "alive and aglow with fruit blossoms and flowers," the verita-
ble "Garden of England," which now grows RAF squadrons to defend
its blessed life. One grass strip suffices for the aircraft, while crew
rooms and offices are dispersed around the fringe, "hidden among the
plum trees of a half cleared orchard. The overall effect was more of a
garden city than an R.A.F. aerodrome" (p. 238). Pierre Closterman's
squadron at Dungeness operates from a sandy spit of land with tents
pitched in an apple orchard, where "The atmosphere was delightful,
more that of a holiday camp or picnic than anything else. You could
stuff yourself with enormous, sweet, juicy apples just by sticking your
arm out through the tent flap" (p. 51).

West Malling's location may be exceptional, but its image of
serene pastoral beauty holds true for most of the fighter stations.
Johnnie Johnson writes with great fondness for Tangmere, "A
pleasant sunny airfield which crouched at the foot of the South
Downs and was only separated from the coast by a small span of flat
Sussex land" (p. 53). The nearby village of Oving provides living
quarters at Rushmans, a fine "old, low rambling house of some
character," which is accepted with great enthusiasm, "for a fighter
squadron is very self-contained and its morale is greatly influenced by
the manner and style in which its members live together" (p. 55).
Bucolic is another term that fits these fields and the images Johnson
and others use to describe them:

> High summer, and the air is heavy with the scent of white
> clover as we lounge in our deck-chairs watching a small tractor
> cut down the long grass on our airfield. In some places it is
> almost a foot high, but it is not dangerous and we know that if
> we are skillful enough to stall our Spitfires just when the tips of
> the grasses caress the wheels then we shall pull off a perfect land-
> ing. (p. 83)

Not just these pilots' lives but their flying tactics are in close touch
with nature, all working in harmony as the squadron's Spitfires rise
and return from the skies like meadowlarks roosting in the grass.

At these forward bases pilots can devote their off-duty hours to a
semblance of the country gentleman's life. Hunting and fishing are
frequent pursuits, usually at the invitation of the local squire, though
in the case of two noncoms in Don Charlwood's crew the business is
common poaching, played right to prowling for partridge, being discovered by the irate farmer, and escaping through the hedge. The

action is considerably more dignified for Richard Hillary and his squadron mates, who hunt grouse on the estate of the Duke of Hamilton, while Cocky Dundas and his Typhoon squadron are quartered in a charming converted mill house near Matlask, where a clear chalk stream stocked with brown trout runs directly beneath their windows. Out on the Broads Johnnie Johnson is taught the lore of wild fowling by "a wonderful old sportsman" (p. 127), and no sooner is the unit moved north than an invitation arrives from Lord Tichfield for a deer shoot in his forest at Berriedale. When forward airfields are established across France in 1944, the pilots discover well-stocked fields unhunted for nearly a half decade, and during duck season, when on patrol, Johnson reconnoiters likely ponds from his Spitfire.

Away from base on leave, RAF pilots and crew habitually stay close to nature, where a walking tour is the most common holiday. Don Charlwood's last break before operational duty is a long climb in Scotland, and his first leave is spent seeking out his family's tucked-away ancestral village, where he is welcomed home as a son. But rambles in the country inevitably bring one to a hilltop, and from there the air war makes its presence felt. For Charlwood the moment is exhilarating, particularly as it forms a link with his vacation world supposedly so far away:

> Outside my window the Exe caressed its stones. I went downstairs and out the door and crossed the bridge into Somerset. Two small boys were fishing intently on the far bank. Behind some cottages I found a lane that led uphill through sunbeams and eddies of gnats. So narrow was it that wagons had touched the hedges on either side, leaving golden stalks of hay among the leaves. I climbed slowly, for I had walked all the afternoon, following the Exe from Tiverton through Cove and Bampton to Exebridge, deviating often through inviting lanes. Now it was 9 o'clock. The lane rose steeply till it brought me to a hilltop with only the sky beyond. Standing there, I heard a faint sound that set my heart pounding and turned my eyes to a veil of cirrus in the west. There, very high, I saw a Lancaster. A surge of pride and strange sorrow swept over me. I stood listening till the sound died, then turned back to Exebridge through the lanes. (p. 159)

Charlwood's journey takes him step by step from pastoral, peacetime England to the air war he flies nightly against Germany; the fact that he can physically trace it and respond with such sympathetic images at all points demonstrates, to us and to himself, the integrity of his role.

For a flier troubled with his job, the images are far less winsome but equally integral, as C. F. Rawnsley, frustrated by his failure to intercept the enemy at night, finds on a hilltop in Cumberland:

> Lying back against the rocks I listened to the soothing, whispered chorus of tiny sounds that we call silence. The wind rustled with a sigh over the rock slabs, and there was a far-off bleating of sheep, and the waters of the becks rushed with an unending and muffled roar down to the sea; and closer at hand there was a clatter of stones and the rings of clinker and triple nob nails striking the good hard rock as a party of walkers came scrambling up across Striding Edge.
>
> And then, almost imperceptibly to all the tiny sounds, there came out of the west a familiar and discordant noise. Reluctantly I opened my eyes and sat up, and I listened to the throb of engines of those faithful old Ansons. And there they were: two A. I. (air interception) training Ansons from Ouston, the target stooging on towards us, the interceptor just behind it, weaving wildly from side to side. I could imagine only too well what was being said on the intercom.
>
> "Hard right . . . steady . . . hard left . . . no . . . right again . . . no . . . Oh . . . it's gone!"
>
> They were hard at it, learning their trade, and even up there in the mountains, safely tucked away in a niche in the rocks, I did not seem to be able to get away from it. (pp. 276–77)

Yet life always brings one back to the RAF station, for there are the loyalties and the familiar, anchoring patterns of existence. These men "are really only happy when they are back with their squadrons, with their associations and memories," Richard Hillary notes. "They long to be back in their planes, so that isolated with the wind and the stars they may play their part in man's struggle against the elements" (p. 49). There is a loyalty among crew, as Lancaster navigator Don Charlwood learns after a particularly harrowing mission when his misplotting the course almost cost them their lives: "I never want to fly with another crew," his pilot announces. "This one will do me" (p. 76). Pilot Jack Currie learns the same lesson when he warns his crew to bail out of their faltering craft before he tries to bring it in: not one soul is willing to leave. High moments such as these are themselves anchored in the secure routine of squadron life, and Charlwood is careful to set the scene for it early in *No Moon Tonight:* the small

village that serves as the station railhead ("the first thing a new arrival saw and, if he survived . . . the last thing he saw as he departed"), the familiar walk or van ride up to the airfield upon returning from leave, the squadron markings that come into view on aircraft parked around the perimeter, the gate, office buildings, and finally the low-ceilinged huts where pilots and crews live and sleep. Along the way there may be farms where the servicemen can work odd jobs during off-hours in exchange for eggs (a treat otherwise reserved for crews returning from missions). Inside the base more ominous details await them, notably the operations chalkboard with assignments for the day or night, prompting a scene Johnnie Johnson records:

> It is fascinating to watch the reactions of the various pilots. They fall into two broad categories: those who are going out to shoot and those who secretly and desperately know they will be shot at, the hunters and the hunted. The majority of pilots, once they have seen their names on the board, walk out to their Spitfires for a pre-flight check and for a word or two with their ground crews. They tie on their mae-wests, check their maps, study the weather forecast and have a last-minute chat with their leaders or wingmen. These are the hunters.
>
> The hunted, that very small minority (although every squadron usually possessed at least one), turned to their escape kits and made sure that they were wearing the tunic with the silk maps sewn into a secret hiding place . . . . When they went through these agonized preparations they reminded me of aged countrywomen meticulously checking their shopping-lists before catching the bus for the market town. (pp. 85–86)

The happiest times at fighter or bomber stations happen away from operations, particularly in the mess. As opposed to their Luftwaffe counterparts, whose free hours are spent in rigorous sporting activities designed to build their stamina for fighting and to strengthen group morale, RAF men choose more rambunctious doings such as bicycle races round the dining tables, planting sooty footprints across the ceiling, rugby scrums among the lounge furniture, and a general topsy-turvy scene in which pilots and crew members throw themselves about with abandon. Away from base the men of the squadron project this image by their behavior and dress. "They get a somewhat malicious pleasure in appearing slightly scruffy when dining at the smartest restaurants," Richard Hillary notes in *The Last*

Enemy, "thus tending to embarrass the beautifully turned out, pink-and-white-cheeked young men of the crack infantry regiments, and making them feel uncomfortably related to choir boys" (p. 48). Even on parade, pilots maintain the tradition of leaving their top tunic button undone and thereby surprise the occasional visitor from another service on dress inspection. But these same qualities have their inverse value when times are bad, as after a particularly costly scramble in *The Big Show* Pierre Closterman remarks of a service club that "The bar is always a gauge of pilots' morale; here it was positively mournful" (p. 150).

The major difference between the RAF and the Luftwaffe experience during the first four years of the war is that the British fliers fight from bases in their home country, whereas the German pilots are stationed on foreign soil and live a more proper military life on occupied airfields. Spitfires and Hurricanes are never more than thirty minutes from England; even the bomber crews, with their night-long missions over enemy territory, bear the schizophrenic pressure of a double life Don Charlwood's *No Moon Tonight* describes so well: "Life on the squadron was seldom far from fantasy. We might, at eight, be in a chair beside a fire, but at ten, in an empty world above a floor of cloud. Or at eight, walking in Barnetby with a girl whose nearness denied all possibility of sudden death at twelve" (p. 77). Charlwood makes much of the airfield's beacon, which is his companion both on walks with his girlfriend and on his return from a mission over Hamburg:

> On a neighboring hill our beacon flashed its red characteristics, its clicking the only sound in the night. It momentarily inflamed a haystack and a cottage wall, then passed them back to darkness.
>
> I remembered that in seven hours I should be waiting for Ted [the bombardier, watching from the Lancaster's nose] to pronounce those blessed words, "Base beacon ahead!" The thought was strange. I pressed Joan's arm and felt her respond. We walked slowly down the hill to the Waafery in the face of a rising wind. At the gate we stood with linked fingers, the feeling of incredulity over us that always comes in these moments. (p. 101)

Charlwood's images follow the metaphorical journey of his story, a narrative in which the peaceful haystack and cottage wall are colored with the incendiary hue of war, a war to which the wind just risen will carry him a few hours hence. Once that trip is undertaken, however, the reality of combat rules his mind until the mission's end, as once more the images of his actual experience make the metaphor real:

> On the familiar order and reply Doug retracts the wheels. Obscure in the failing light I can see the village. Somewhere among the huddled buildings the girl of the fair, upswept hair is listening. That we stood so close an hour ago I can scarcely believe. We are in cloud; now out of it; now deeply into the main layer. We are wrapped about in mists that erase from our minds all sense of whereabouts. To me we have become nothing more than a mark on the white expanse of my chart, which we shall remain until the journey is over. (p. 110)

An important feature of these stories is how their particulars of lyric description and even narrative action grow from the qualities of life at hand, reaching from station routine and proximity to home all the way to the exhilaration of flight and the terrors of battle. Bob Braham begins *"Scramble!"* with words on the startling contrast between the chaos of combat, when he and his colleagues take off to fight for their lives and for their country's existence, and the near-normal circumstances they return to "among a civilian population, often in quiet villages and small towns, which war had not hit and where life remained calm. Many of us came back to wife and children and our own home as, for long periods, I did. We drank with the locals in English pubs an hour, perhaps, after a fantastic escape or a hazardous victory" (p. 15). Such proximity to home can make a lost combat an especially heartbreaking affair, as Douglas Bader discovers as he lies in hospital near the Luftwaffe base at St. Omer thinking of the dinner date with his wife and the foursome of golf planned for the next day. For wives and girlfriends the closeness can be very hard to bear, as it is for a Waaf on duty at the squadron chalkboard, unable to bring herself to record her fiancé's missing Lancaster yet obliged to remain at her station to the embarrassment of all. Even the small social niceties take their toll. When a mission to Dunkirk interrupts a sherry party organized for a fighter squadron and their wives, no one is willing to cancel, even after two pilots are reported lost and their wives slip away discreetly from the waiting party.

The prospect of taking on the Luftwaffe by day and returning to one's "slippers and the fire in the evening," as Douglas McRoberts puts it in *Lions Rampant* (p. 87), generates its share of irony. A ten-day leave for every six weeks on duty, with the furlough often spent at home, tends to raise eyebrows among civilians who assume their safety is being ensured by savage fighting "at the front." The air war, of course, erases any such notion of battle lines and combat zones, but its random distribution and touch-and-go nature keep all but a few target areas clear of the fighting.

The strength of these contrasts is shown by Dennis Knight's *Harvest of Messerschmitts,* an interpolation of the diary of Mary Smith, a villager from Elham in Kent, with Knight's own account of the events at nearby RAF Hawkinge, one of the Battle of Britain's most active and vulnerable fighter stations. At times Miss Smith's entries are comic in their understatement, as when she writes: "22 June. Scharnhorst hit and damaged. First green peas" (p. 54). But more often they create an interesting counterpoint between the waging of war and the living of one's life in peace. For a millenium England had, at least domestically, responded to foreign war by withdrawing into its geographic isolation, but now in 1940 a pastoral valley such as Elham "was suddenly in the front line" (p. 9). From Hawkinge, on a clear day, one can see France, and from there the Stukas and Messerschmitts threaten. The villagers have their war spirit, but even its tendency toward the ridiculous, as when Miss Peggy Prince sets out in her canoe to rescue the pilot of a ditched bomber, resolves itself in the sublime, as the man's life is saved and Miss Prince is awarded the Order of the British Empire. Some Hawkinge pilots are local boys from Kent, and when Sergeant Geof Goodman of Horley downs a Messerschmitt 110 he buzzes his home with a series of victory rolls, stirring the townsfolk to "wave sheets and towels at him" (p. 113). This part of Kent is witness to countless battles, and the title of Knight's book indicates the harvest of wrecked German planes gathered in salvage dumps such as the one hidden on the outskirts of Elham. But the greatest thrills come from the chase and the kill, which happen virtually in the villagers' laps:

> The Palmers stood transfixed, each inwardly thinking that the wailing plane above [a crashing Messerschmitt 109] was going to fall on them and there was nothing they could do to escape it. The children, John and Tina, though toddlers, watched with the same fascination as the plane grew larger and larger and the noise increased until it filled the whole valley with sound. Luckily it fell past them down into the valley, and they had a magnificent view as it exploded, sending up a ball of orange and black fire that silenced the terrible screaming that had filled their heads. A

single Spitfire came up the valley low, flashing light and dark as
it executed an impeccable roll over the burning wreck and causing the villagers' hearts to swell with pride. (p. 154)

Once again the iconography of battle is present for all to see and
for the writer to incorporate as the structuring center of his memoir.
Proximity to home is a favorite element, whether for dogfights or
homelike behavior, and even when on base the self-described "RAF
types" delight in raffish, unsophisticated activity. When Flight Lieutenant Ginger Lacey is surprised by no less a figure than King George
VI, who has joined their squadron mess to congratulate the pilot for
bringing down the Heinkel that had bombed Buckingham Palace, he
unself-consciously offers the monarch a drink and promptly orders
two beers, to the horror of the sherry-drinking VIPs; yet, as Douglas
McRoberts reports, "His Majesty drank his half-pint without hesita-
tion" (p. 166). When fighter sweeps are mounted over France, Group
Captain Findlay Boyd chooses to shoot up a hotel which had thrown
him out on a summer holiday in 1938. For fighter pilots, who very
often operate over the villages and lanes they travel by auto or by foot
each day, air combat has this personal flavor, which at times spills
over as comedy.

Quite different is the abstract world of bomber crews, whose
occasional low-altitude approaches to their targets bring them so close
that, as Don Charlwood notes, "we could have spoken to people in
the streets." Yet this nearness only "accentuates the feeling of fantasy
that often came to me, the feeling of being so near yet so very far
from the hidden life of Europe" (p. 72). *Bomber Pilot,* written by
Leonard Cheshire early in the war, reveals the flier enjoying a bird's-
eye view of both his father's home in Oxford and the street where he
had lived in Berlin. Cheshire remarks how odd it is, when taking off
on a bomb run, to fly over a village pub at dusk and wonder about the
night ahead for the pubgoers (as opposed to his own night over Germany) only to return home after several hours in the maelstrom of
searchlights, flak, and night fighters for debriefing and a late Bing
Crosby film with the locals.

A unique approach to the war's relative proximity characterizes
the memoirs of expatriate pilots. In editor Victor Houart's transcript,
*Lonely Warrior: The Journal of Battle of Britain Fighter Pilot Jean
Offenberg,* the young Belgian airman's first combat experience takes
place as his country is overrun, and it is a telling point when he pulls

out of a dogfight with two Messerschmitts to find himself over "the little town of Diest, the home of dark sweet beer which one drank in big pewter pots" (p. 17). From the vantage point of history we know he will never see this town or taste its beer again, for within a day his Belgian squadron will retreat to France. His own escape to Morocco and journey to England wins him back his wings and the chance to fly Hurricanes and Spitfires from the last months of the Battle of Britain to January 22, 1942, when he is killed in a flying accident. It is an emotional moment when from the air he first sees the coast of France, which is "almost home" (p. 90). Like the French pilots flying under a nom de guerre, Offenberg must wonder if the people at home regard him as a deserter or a potential liberator—a vexing question, because Belgium is at once so near and so far, only thirty minutes away by Spitfire. But in reality his homeland is years away—the three years until the Allied invasion, which the fated flier will never live to see. By July 8, 1941, the new offensive policy of fighter sweeps and bomber cover brings him to twenty-eight thousand feet above the coast of the Continent, from where he can see the Zuider Zee. "Pity I couldn't work over Belgium," he notes in his diary. "What would I not give to make a landing outside Brussels" (p. 157), near his home. But because for now he no longer has a home, he fights all the more intently to end the war, with the same spirit as the equally aggressive Poles, Czechs, Dutch, Norwegians, and Frenchmen, who are anxious to reclaim their nations.

The classic case of a foreign flier pushing RAF limits is that of the Frenchman, described in Bobby Oxspring's *Spitfire Command,* who has no patience for a tractor-mower obstructing the grass runway at Hawkinge where he wishes to land. "Bawling French obscenities over the R/T [radiotelephone] at Flying Control," Oxspring notes, "he retracted his wheels and fired a short burst of machine gun fire some yards ahead of the tractor. The terrified driver lit for parts unknown while the tractor steered itself off the airfield" (p. 106). Only an expatriate eager to return home, the author observes, could get away with something like that. But Oxspring finds a similar ironic humor in how the war is brought home to his own squadron, based near London at Kenley. When one day they find themselves released from operations, they spend it at East London's greyhound track. Soon the seats at Catford stadium provide front row seats for a Luftwaffe attack on the docks—the most massive German raid of the war. As the 350 bombers escorted by over 600 fighters are harried by 20 squadrons of Hurricanes and Spitfires while beneath them miles of dockland burn and the Woolwich Arsenal explodes, the off-duty pilots cheer their comrades and the stalwart Londoners lay down bets as the races proceed on schedule.

The intimacy of station life and its proximity to home makes the loss of colleagues especially hard to bear. But bear them the fliers must, since a high rate of attrition is written into their service lives. Tony Dudgeon, whose posting in the Middle East keeps him out of the earlier European air battles, estimates in *The Luck of the Devil* that the chances of a pilot surviving from the Battle of Britain to the German surrender were less than one in seven. Bomber crews are up against worse odds, pledged to thirty operations while facing a loss rate of 5 percent, meaning that any man past twenty has outlived the average, yet with ten ops to go. Don Charlwood's *No Moon Tonight* accepts these losses as a matter of daily life. From his navigator's table at preflight briefings he sees his counterpart from nearly every other crew go missing, "from some tables three or four navigators, from others more" (p. 62). Surviving such odds is more than luck, for the fortunate souls who beat the averages must live with their squadron's losses, a fact that can break a flier's nerve unless he adopts a "so it goes" attitude toward death. In fact, death becomes as routine as the mail delivery:

> When we rose, the men who had gone on the flap were sleeping, but news of them had already reached us. One crew was missing. We remembered them vaguely from the night before, chiefly because one of their number had grumbled at the lack of Australian mail. There was mail for him now, but by lunch time it had been taken from the rack. That was all there was to it. Scarcely a ripple on the surface of the station's life. (pp. 20–21)

The closer quarters of squadron operations make such deaths harder on the fighter pilots, for they have most likely breakfasted with their colleague and an hour later seen him disappear in flames, his empty place at the evening mess table a brutal reminder of the event. The routines of station life extend to the ground crews, who are personally responsible for their planes and emotionally involved in their fates. They speak quite naturally about "bedding down" the Spitfires each night, chocking the wheels and covering the cockpits, as if they were tucking in a child. When a plane fails to return, the bed is left empty. In Johnnie Johnson's *Wing Leader* ten of twelve fighters are retired for the night by their dutiful ground crews — "all except the crews of the two missing Spitfires, who stood apart in a restless, disconsolate little group and who occasionally fell silent and strained their eyes to the east, as if peering hard enough they would see their two Spitfires swinging in to land" (pp. 101–2).

As common and fateful as they are, losses occupy only a fraction of a squadron's time, just as combat itself exists for only a few manic seconds set within hours and sometimes days of boredom. Yet no memoirists dwell on the tedious aspects of station life; a more common scene away from the fighting is the pleasant idyll of living in such rare circumstances, a picture that cannot help but conjure images of Arthurian knights at ease. In *Duel of Eagles* Peter Townsend recalls the first day of war, not in a mood of hostility or even anxiety but rather of peacefulness, "lying beside my Hurricane watching flaky white clouds drift across a blue sky, while hovering larks shrilled and voices came to me from pilots and ground crew also lying beside their dispersed aircraft. Never in my life had I experienced so peaceful a scene" (p. 191). As essential as the fighter's talents for describing combat is his sensitivity to nuances of peace and beauty; whether British or German, the writer always has an eye for the poetic, even as he goes about his deadly work.

The finest poetry in these memoirs is occasioned by moments of flight. A pilot's preparation takes place within a context laden with sensations, from the sight of an airfield on alert to the comforting smells of aircraft dope, fine mineral oil, and high-grade fuel. A take-off from Tangmere prompts a special thrill in Johnnie Johnson's narrative voice, even when he recalls it fifteen years later:

> We slant into the clean sky. No movement in the cockpit except the slight trembling of the stick as if it is alive and not merely the focal point of a superb mechanical machine. Gone are the ugly tremors of apprehension which plagued us just before the take-off. Although we are sealed in our tiny cockpits and separated from each other, the static from our radios pours through the earphones of our tightly fitting helmets and fills our ears with reassuring crackles. When the leader speaks, his voice is warm and vital, and we know that we are now bound together by a deeper intimacy than we can ever feel on the ground. Invisible threads of trust and comradeship hold us together and the mantle of Bader's leadership will sustain and protect us throughout the fight ahead. The Tangmere Wing is together. (pp. 87–88)

It is not just Johnson's aircraft but his language that comes to life as he and his colleagues head out on their fighter sweep. The adjective *slant* becomes an active verb, taking them into a realm cleansed of earthly improprieties. The plane's feeling of animation comforts Johnson as only a sense of life can, just as the radio's static takes on humanly communicative force. When the wing leader does speak, the already transcended finitude of machine and radio assumes even greater proportions, as the human voice binds all the fliers body and soul with the promise of triumph and survival. Johnson's description itself animates the paragraph's final sentence, for not until all of its sensations are expressed can the Tangmere Wing be said to be in action.

Johnson's enemies are equally sensitive to the poetry of flight. In *The Diving Eagle* Luftwaffe pilot Peter Stahl tells of flying his Junkers 88 on missions to England at the time when Bader's wing was hunting them. Stahl's voice speaks more of the solitude of flight, as his bomber is often alone over Britain with just the elements for company. But just as Johnson vitalizes his control stick and radio, Stahl responds to features of the weather in language far beyond the routine associations of life on the ground, even when he flies an obsolete Dornier on a courier mission:

> The Dornier continues climbing bravely and then it becomes obvious that the sunlight will soon break through; the thick murk pulls past the cabin in more and more uneven swathes, then there are only tattered bits of clouds, and suddenly the sunshine reflects off the instrument panel. We are through!
> I can breathe easily again and take my eyes off the instruments, to enjoy that ever-fascinating image when an aircraft surfaces out of the clouds into the radiant lightness and endless solitude of the cloud scenery. At this time the eyes see only two colors, the saturated, indescribably beautiful blue of the sky that fades only a shade towards the horizon, and the blinding whiteness of the clouds. On these occasions I am always ever more impressed by the limitless extent and solitude one leaps into so suddenly, an experience that is overwhelming even though it has become more or less a daily event. (pp. 34–35)

Much later, in a night attack against Greenock on the Clyde in Scotland, Stahl takes time to orient his narrative to visual sensations prompted by the weather, noting how "The cloud cover beneath us is still unbroken, lit up by searchlights from underneath. This creates an effect of flying over a giant pane of frosted glass" (p. 153). Disorientation inspires its own poetry, and Stahl is amused by his own panic at the sight of "a fiery red spot growing visibly larger right ahead of us" (p. 97) amid the night defenses of London, an apparition that proves to be nothing but the rising moon. Even the destruction wrought by Stahl's incendiaries commands the attention of language; because it "defies description," he is compelled to circle around a second time and study the "gruesome spectacle" (p. 101). As conscious as he is of the suffering below, he cannot help but cast the scene in technological terms, describing the "airspace" as "a giant fireball" (p. 82). As Johnson animated the inanimate to evoke the fighter adventure, so Stahl abstracts the destructiveness of his bomber into a matter of light and combustion, the same pattern that distinguishes fighter and bomber narratives about closeness to life on the ground. Each technique allows the flier to face the challenges of his work, whether in the air or on the page.

As squadron life has its rhythms on the ground, so flight operations yield their own counterpoint of action and relief. Johnson, like all fighter pilots, dwells on the eerie emptiness of sky that follows by seconds the most frantically crowded combat, and Stahl speaks fondly of the aftermath of a bombing run, when he turns his Junkers 88 to the southeast, throttles back the engines and settles in for a shallow glide home. "All of a sudden everything is quiet around us and the fireworks are left behind," and with tension easing it is possible to rethink the action just concluded in terms now much larger than life. "We live through again the minutes after our attack when we came out of the defensive circle and the aircraft was light as a bird. We enjoy these moments as if experiencing the world for the first time" (p. 104). To flavor the sensation he turns to his traditional treat on the homeward journey—a sandwich and coffee—a routine shared by his adversaries in the Lancaster squadrons, which three years hence would be pounding Germany each night.

In the Lancaster bombers air force life assumes its most intimate dimensions, as the seven crew members work in close harmony, virtually detached from their fellow men and women on the ground. Don Charlwood describes this effect as a mission begins: "Whatever we may be in other hours, in this moment of take-off, as we part from the earth, a different spirit holds us" (p. 109). In his crewmates' voices he can hear the realization, "called out by the intensity of the hour," that theirs is a special world; each voice reveals "an awareness of his life for the men with him and, more than this, a moment of widened vision in which all danger, and death itself, assume their ultimate proportions, which are far less than the proportions we have given them in daily life" (pp. 109–10). This very special sensation is shared each time the ground crew closes the door and seals them in their fuselage to fly another mission. Coupled with the tender moments he shares with his Waaf girlfriend, such spirit prompts him to wish that his life at the bomber station "might go on forever. The unattainable thirty was something of no consequence" (p. 95).

What of the individuals? Although there were plenty of fliers who cut a noteworthy figure, their most dominant traits of personality emerge in harmony with the squadron tone. Even Douglas Bader, one of the most individualistic pilots to survive the war, earns his greatest fame as a team man, from his organization of the "big wings" to his ability to keep a squadron at its peak of confidence. Johnnie Johnson's reputation is much the same as he draws praise for getting discouraged and decimated units back on their feet and fighting effectively again. The war's most outrageous pilot, the Canadian flier Buzz "Screwball" Beurling, shows poorly against Johnson when the wing leader gives him a stern rebuke for leaving the formation and hunting on his own. Beurling's story, as told by Brian Nolan in *Hero: The Falcon of Malta,* is a sad one. Rejected by the Canadian and British air forces both before and after the war, he succeeds only as a self-styled misfit among the outnumbered, ragtag airmen on Malta. When he returns to England, where the fighting is more disciplined, he finds heroism is accorded in a different fashion, as Johnnie Johnson explains:

> I said that the days of the lone wolf went out with the First World War, and, as far as I was concerned, they had never formed any part of our doctrine in this war over Britain and Occupied Europe. Screwball Beurling had demonstrated over Malta that an aggressive, single-handed fighter pilot could knock down a reasonable bag of enemy aircraft, given the opportunities and a fair share of luck. No pilot, though, however skillful, could consistently shoot down aircraft and guard his own tail at the same time. I went to some lengths to emphasize that I was not decrying Beurling's exploits but simply stating that I could not countenance single-handed exploits in my own outfit. We fought as a team, and if the circumstances broke up the team and its members found themselves alone, then, to use a descriptive Canadian phrase, "we got the hell out of it." (p. 198)

Turning Beurling's own language against him, Johnson sets the tone for the successful fighter pilot personality, with which Beurling's own personality cannot harmonize. The hero of Malta soon gets the hell out himself, to pursue a life of controversy in Canada; he dies in mysterious circumstances flying across the Atlantic to join the Israeli Air Force in 1948. Bader, on the other hand, rallies his disheartened fliers with cheers for anticipated combat and gives the just-met Johnson "a profound impression of the qualities of leadership displayed in a moment of tension by the assertive squadron leader" (p. 28).

Having established their fame within the proper guidelines of squadron life, the fliers with high awards—the Distinguished Service Order, the Distinguished Flying Cross, and the Victoria Cross (Guy Gibson was decorated with this rare medal)—move as apparitions through each other's books. Al Deere speculates in *Nine Lives* that he may be one of the pilots the newly arrived Bader is described as gazing at "in mild derision" (p. 59). Johnnie Johnson's squadron loudly celebrates their recently won commendations in a London pub and are kiddingly greeted as "glamor boys" by the much quieter—and more highly decorated—Guy Gibson (*Wing Leader,* pp. 153–54). Soon after the war Johnson meets the Luftwaffe ace and fighter commander Adolf Galland and is impressed with the man's "quiet dignity and his unshakable faith in his own tactics and theories" (p. 74), two qualities that emerge nine years later in Galland's *The First and the Last.*

Even apparitions draw criticism when they violate good squadron practice. Peter Townsend (*Duel of Eagles*) takes the legendary Richard Hillary (*The Last Enemy*) to task for attaching his Spitfire, with its different speed, tactics, and radio wavelength, to Townsend's flight of Hurricanes over Dungeness. In Hillary's book the affair is comic; he jokes about having got himself "shot down acting as 'Arse-end-Charlie' to a squadron of Hurricanes" (p. 111). But Townsend is the better man at tactics and realizes that Hillary, by putting himself astern in an aircraft that from the rear can be mistaken for a Messerschmitt Me109, veils the Hurricanes from the threat of an actual Me109 sneaking up from behind to shoot down Townsend's wingman. Hillary goes on to crash-land harmlessly in the midst of a brigade cocktail party, where he is toasted with double whiskies. Townsend's report is cryptic, a text more appropriate to the actuality of war: " 'If this Spitfire pilot can be identified, I would like these facts brought home to him, because his . . . action contributed to the loss of one of my flight commanders' " (p. 375). One last indiscretion proves to be Hillary's undoing, and it too is recorded in another man's memoir, C. F. Rawnsley's *Night Fighter.* "Hillary was a man who apparently had every kind of courage but the sort needed to go to his Commanding Officer and admit that night flying was too much for him," Rawnsley confides, after reading the young man's letters detailing "the tragic struggle that went on in his mind" (p. 203). Fate soon catches up with the troubled young pilot. "Just after midnight on the 7th of January [1943] his aircraft, a Blenheim, which had been orbiting a flashing beacon, was seen to spiral down and crash, and Hillary was killed" (p. 203).

If death becomes problematic in these texts, love is even more so. Nearly every memoir devotes appreciable space to the protagonist's romantic life during the war years — most often a relationship that leads to marriage and a life lived happily ever after, less frequently a love all trace of which vanishes along with squadron life at the end of the war. But in every story these relationships take second place to the writer's involvement with the RAF.

The love stories in the narratives usually begin with the same suddenness of meeting, a pure matter of chance, which nevertheless rivets attention. In Bob Braham's case, the moment comes on a night in town: "That evening in Simon's Bar in the Grand Hotel I espied a beautiful girl sitting at a table with an older woman. To the annoyance of the girl-friend beside me, I couldn't take my eyes off this new attraction" (p. 66). Don Charlwood is out for a pleasant evening at The Berkley in Scunthorpe when he first sees his future love across the room in a group of Waafs, and even at this distance he takes her measure well: "I noticed that her eyes were animated and gay while she was speaking to others, but in repose, grave and almost lonely" (p. 51). Jack Currie's *Mosquito Victory* shows the author using air tactics to win the affections of the Waaf he admires; he flies her to a new station in London and makes her think she is holding the flight controls. But even this episode in their relationship must wait until after the systematic account of their first meeting. "The new girl's eyes were wide-set and merry. She smiled, and gave me an open, friendly gaze; friendly, but appraising — the gaze of a girl who has indeed heard all, if not to say too much, about a man" (p. 15). In all three scenes the noted details become functional within the narrative that follows: Braham's social indiscretions, which form the basis of his sudden but lasting romance; Charlwood's deep appraisal of the qualities that will anchor not just his affection but his introspective approach to service life among the rhythms of combat and leave; and the playful, sometimes reckless, but always engaging manner in which Currie tells his story, not just of love but of the whole war. In the best of these memoirs, the love story is never extraneous, but helps structure events and enhance the tone, from Braham's unconventionality and Charlwood's broodings to Currie's snappy, even saucy narrative.

Love stories can also have a comic dimension. Johnnie Johnson's account of his relationship with his fiancée (and later wife) Paula almost always shares the page with stories of his Labrador puppy, Sally, whom he inevitably treats better. The ninth chapter of *Wing Leader* ends with a goodbye to Paula, as Johnson's new rank takes him to a distant command without her. When she asks why his promotion cannot be delayed, he offers no answer; across the page the very next chapter begins with her husband driving off to Kenley "with Sally the Labrador curled up beside me" (p. 137). Johnson's last mention of wife and dog together signals a development common to all RAF memoirs, that of the secondary place family life takes to flying and to the war:

> Paula and I spent two weeks together before I took over my new appointment on the planning staff of 11 Group headquarters. In Norfolk we walked the root fields together after a few partridges. Sally worked well, and although we got a few birds I suspected that my young wife was not much interested in the sport. She regarded the despatch of wounded birds with some horror, and my dream of happy days together with Paula shouldering a light sporting gun began to evaporate. Sally limped toward me with a thorn in her foot, so I handed my twelve bore to Paula and knelt down to remove the thorn. Suddenly there was a loud bang and the Labrador and I were peppered with earth and bits of sugar beet. It was my closest shave of the war and marked my wife's last appearance in the shooting-field! (p. 170)

It is also her last appearance of any substance in the narrative, as Johnson returns his attention to the more rewarding world of combat flying, where he can hunt bravely, offer succor as needed to boon companions, and not be gunned down by a wife.

Richard Hillary is one of the few memoirists to remain single, death taking him before romance is allowed to bloom, but his conscious choice anticipates a mood underlying most other accounts:

> I didn't believe that a man with something important to do in this war wanted the responsibility of a wife, more especially if he loved her. She was a distracting liability and he would be far

happier with her out of the way. Then he could concentrate his whole mind on his job without having to wonder the whole time whether she was safe. All he needed was the purely physical satisfaction of some woman, and that he could get anywhere. (p. 73)

The tone of these comments fits the cynical style of *The Last Enemy*'s earlier chapters, before Hillary's insights into the compassion of war and the heroism of peace.

Bob Braham confesses that he shares some of these sentiments. He writes that when transferred away from his new wife "I soon forgot my disappointment for I knew we should be in the thick of it. I doubt whether Joan could have understood my thoughts. But I was still very young and the RAF was my first love" (p. 68). He admits to being "very selfish. The RAF came first and my wife and family second" (p. 87), and his growing responsibilities as Squadron Commander leave even less time for home, since he feels obliged to lead by example. The conflict between duties reaches an extreme when the air-raid sirens wail and he interrupts his leave to phone a nearby airfield and borrow a Beaufighter. "Joan was angry. I had only come home for two days and here I was trying to go off flying again. I must admit it was most selfish" (p. 112). Every leave is like this, for "in some perverse way, after a day with the family I felt I had to get back with my comrades. Relaxing in Leicester filled me with a sense of guilt when I knew other members of my outfit were fighting it out against the enemy" (p. 142). Squadron life dominates the family circle, to the point that Braham gets irritated with his small children. "My squadron was everything to me, more even than my wife and family" (p. 159), he admits, and because the two realms will not mix, he decides to live apart. Even at this moment his love for the RAF shows through; in the paragraph where he announces this regretful decision Braham soon turns to words of admiration for his new staff and appreciation of their "example, leadership, and fantastic pranks" (p. 170).

Braham's prejudice is not unique to the RAF, for the joys of squadron life also form an important part of Peter Stahl's Luftwaffe memoir, *The Diving Eagle*. A commercial weather pilot who is not happy to have both his career and marriage interrupted by military service, Stahl nevertheless admits that "Despite all the joys of home leave and living with my own family I felt a real homesickness for my

Staffel [squadron] and friends there. I kept watching the weather and following the High Command communiqués to have some idea of what life in Gilze [his station] must be like" (p. 105).

British and German fliers feel this way for an obvious reason: life on squadron duty, thanks to its complete network of supports and relationships undertaken in the heightened atmosphere of imminent death, has replaced home and family as the vital center of their lives. Its artifice only makes it that more effective as a pleasing, rewarding surrogate for the peacetime style of existence. Consider the contrast between the discord in Bob Braham's family, a life of "aggravation, often leading to heated arguments . . . about the bringing up of the children" (p. 182), and the joy Richard Hillary takes in a group of evacuated Scottish children near his base in Tarfside, with whom he and his squadron mates spend hours picnicking and playing piggyback, rounders, and hide-and-seek. Even on operations the fliers keep a place in their hearts for the children, so easy for them to do in these artificial circumstances away from the hard realities of actual family relations:

> The legend of the children at Tarfside soon spread through the Squadron, and no three machines would return from a practice flight without first sweeping in tight formation low along the bed of the valley where the children, grouped on a patch of grass by the road, would wave and shout and dance in ecstasy. (p. 84)

Unlike Braham, who comes to welcome moves away from his family, the transfer south of Hillary's unit is a sentimental affair for both pilots and children. "They had heard the news," he writes, "and as we went into line astern and dived one by one in salute over the valley, none of the children moved or shouted. With white boulders they had spelt out on the road the two words: 'Good Luck' " (p. 97).

4
The Fighter Style

I N the iconography of modern warfare few images are more deeply etched than that of the Spitfire squadron scrambling across a grassy airfield and rising to the skies. The picture is most certainly an ikon, for in films produced from the war years through the late 1960s a spectacular set of film clips was used again and again, until it became an object of veneration as much as representation. Shot by a Twentieth Century Fox film crew at Prestwick for *A Yank in the RAF*, 602 Squadron's scramble and mock dogfights turned out so photographically perfect that they were used repeatedly in films from the wartime *Mrs. Miniver* and *Dangerous Moonlight* to *The Battle of Britain* in 1969. The image of these scrambling fighter squadrons fits perfectly the reality, since the sight of twelve fighters at a moment's notice bouncing across a forward airfield to intercept their adversaries before the target combines the major factors that set the style for this war.

Consider the planes and their performance. With a top speed close to four hundred miles per hour, an effective fighting ceiling exceeding thirty thousand feet, and an armament (initially eight machine guns, then with cannons mixed in) capable of downing a large bomber in two to four seconds of fire, these Spitfires (and their cousin, the Hurricane) represent a quantum leap in aircraft development, for only two years before, their pilots were flying lightly armed biplanes built for scarcely half the speed that looked much more a part of the war of 1918 than of the brave new world of 1940. In Spitfires and Hurricanes pilots could do things undreamed of just a few years earlier; as a result, the book of fighter tactics written in the 1920s and 1930s had to be quickly revised under fire. The presence of these planes had a decisive effect on the war's overall strategy, for had Germany launched air attacks against England in 1938 or even 1939 the RAF simply would not have had adequate and appropriate forces to repel them. But by 1940, although the odds were still unfavorable, at least the numbers were there to guarantee a game, so that even a mere twelve fighters scrambling against fifty or a hundred or more bombers stood a chance of thwarting the attack.

The German attacks themselves were another factor previously unexperienced in air warfare, although a textbook for them did exist: General Giulio Douhet's *The Command of the Air,* which since 1921 had presented a plan for winning wars by destroying a nation's capacity to fight through massive and relentless bombing of its economic facilities as well as military targets. Although in mid summer of 1940 Göring's forces were directed against both Channel shipping and the RAF (on the ground and in the air), developments of late August caused Hitler to revise the air strategy and turn against London and various provincial cities instead. Revenge for the August 25, 1940, bombing of Berlin, itself an RAF reprisal for a Luftwaffe raid that strayed over London, was one motive, but Douhet's thinking was also evident in Hitler's decision: perhaps this way the previously elusive RAF could be tempted into more open battle, and Great Britain's ability to wage war could be frustrated by destroying its transportation, factories, and workers' housing. Those twelve scrambling Spitfires take to the air to combat a revolutionary new style of aggression.

A third pertinent factor is evident in their scramble. No Luftwaffe bombers can be seen or even be heard, but the twelve pilots know from where the attack is coming, including how many aircraft and at what altitude, thanks to another innovation: early-warning radar. In place less than a year by 1940, this remarkable defense system was linked with a comprehensive network of alert and control, so that bombers forming up over France and turning to cross the Channel could be plotted as their missions began; orders could be sent from Group Command to sector stations and from there to the individual squadrons and eventually to the pilots in their planes, rallying and directing a defense for airfields and cities.

Together these factors set the terms on which the air war would be fought, and its striking point was the scrambling squadron pictured so dramatically in countless films and photographs from the war years to the present. In *Fighter* Len Deighton adopts a revealing historical perspective, explaining that "The internal combustion engine, the aeroplane and wireless transformed war even more than gunpowder or steam-power had done. But during the twentieth century only one great battle has been fought and decided by these three inventions alone, and that was the Battle of Britain" (p. 114).

A battle in three dimensions, moving at high speed—this is Deighton's characterization of the fighter war, which aptly describes the fighter style and spirit. Luftwaffe formations would fly in over Britain as many as five deep: Stuka dive-bombers on the bottom, Junkers or Dornier or Heinkel medium bombers above them, surrounded by Messerschmitt 110 destroyers, plus a level of Messerschmitt 109 fighters to protect the Me110s, all complemented by another group of Me109s ranging free on top. Facing them would be a squadron or wing of Spitfires to draw off the Me109s and leave the more vulnerable Me110s and bombers for the attacking Hurricanes. The size of these engagements became massive, with the Germans flying 1,176 sorties on August 15, 1940, and nearly the same number the next day. Of these missions 120 ended in lost aircraft for the Germans, who destroyed only 62 British planes both in the air and on the ground. Tilting the balance even more in favor of the British was the fact that only 21 RAF pilots were lost, whereas the Air Ministry made the inflated but at the time credible claim that 225 German planes had been shot down and most of their crews (as many as four men in a bomber) killed or captured. This was a strong propaganda victory, important for maintaining domestic morale and American support. The most remarkable aspect of this combat, however, was that despite the high speed and massive numbers, every individual action could be plotted and accounted for: the 816 tightly printed pages of Winston G. Ramsey's *The Battle of Britain Then and Now* list each engagement that led to an RAF or Luftwaffe casualty, a record of knightly combat worthy of Arthurian legend.

It was the fighter style that lent air combat this sense of individuality. Not only were planes such as the Spitfire, Hurricane, Messerschmitt, and Focke-Wulf a world apart from the medium and heavy bombers that conducted the other phase of the air war, but the pilots who flew them were a notably separate breed. A bomber needs from four to seven men to fly it, each with an assigned task drawing upon a specific talent—piloting, flight engineering, navigation, radio communication, bomb aiming, and the various modes of gunnery. The kind of flier drawn to such work was a different person from the fighter pilot, a distinction made as early as the first weeks of training, for bomber service was the choice of pilot trainees set to pursue a career in civil aviation, who needed multiengine instruction to qualify for such employment.

The fighter pilots' independence extends to their behavior on the job and their care of their equipment. No fighter fresh off the assembly line seems comfortable enough for a pilot like Douglas Bader or Johnnie Johnson, and throughout the war their memoirs record them making small and sometimes large adjustments to their Hurricanes and Spitfires so that the aircraft's performance will fit their own style of fighting. During the Battle of France, when the fighter squadrons are taking heavy punishment in the air, British pilots balk at their planes' lack of defensive armor. To correct the problem they strip the metal linings from the seatbacks of crashed Defiants and Battles and install them in their own fighters; the added weight causes no appreciable loss in performance, and factories are soon following the pilots' improvised solution. By the time of the Battle of Britain experienced pilots no longer accept the standard ranging of guns at maximum distance and instead reset the synchronization themselves at less than one-third the range in order to concentrate their firepower—another tactic soon adopted as official procedure. When a new Spitfire model adds cannons, Bader declines it and keeps his old aircraft, insisting that the heavier ordnance inspires sloppy shooting. In high-speed maneuvering the Spitfire becomes especially hard to control, and as airspeed reaches above four hundred miles per hour the ailerons can hardly be moved. When the pilots discover that the cause of the problem is that the ailerons are made of fabric, they refit their machines with metal control surfaces even before factory conversions can be scheduled. With their planes rearmored, guns readjusted, and ailerons replaced, the RAF fighter pilots improvise their own procedures for attack. They habitually add several thousand feet to their controllers' plots to assure a height advantage. Douglas Bader rallies separate squadrons together to form larger wings, a practice he would argue directly to his commanding officer at Group headquarters and to the Air Staff itself.

These nuances of the fighter style complement the overall technical advance in high-speed, highly armed single-seat aircraft, which by 1940 had swung the tide against the bomber. As late as 1936 strategic thinking still held that thanks to its superior speed and greater numbers "the bomber will always get through," as was surely the case with the Luftwaffe's Condor Legion in Spain. The planning shift came in 1937, in the midst of the Spanish Civil War, when the new British minister for coordination of defense, Sir Thomas Inskip, realized that his country simply could not outrun Germany in the bomber race. There were already too many Heinkels and Dorniers in the air for England to fight a bombing war of attrition, and to counter the

Luftwaffe's plan of a sudden and overwhelming knockout of British resources, Inskip decided the RAF would do better to launch a stand-off defense with fighters while Britain's allies rallied to supply and support it in a longer war. Here the race was winnable, for fighters cost far less to build than bombers, and the recent development of radar suggested they could be deployed with maximum effectiveness. Fighters offered speed, efficiency, and rational direction to a war which otherwise promised to be an uncivilized and indiscriminate slaughter. Inskip's decision not only formed the war's central ikon—the fighter—but determined the style of its success in symbolizing Britain's victory in this phase of the war.

The fighter pilots were quick to develop a flying style appropriate to this strategy and befitting its image. Motivation came from the very top, as Air Chief Marshal Dowding, the leader of Fighter Command, implemented Inskip's strategy of preventing a knockout blow by devising tactics that allowed his archetypal fighter pilot to "scheme like a fox," in Allen Andrews's words (p. 54). Such thinking became the idée fixe of the entire Battle of Britain: the master at Uxbridge cleverly rotating his strength, the squadron leaders calling "Tally-Ho!", and the individual pilot struggling to outsmart the "hunters' squadron" (*Jägerstaffel*) of Messerschmitts. From Dowding came the directive that commenced development of the Hurricane and Spitfire, both of them based on the performance features of the award-winning Supermarine seaplanes: low-wing, all-metal, high-speed monoplanes that would change fighter combat for nearly a half-century (only the high-tech electronics of the 1970s would reduce fighter warfare to an abstract if deadly arcade game). Knowing when *not* to fight was a large part of Dowding's genius. He rejected the Luftwaffe's gambit to draw all his squadrons to France in May 1940 or to force his reserves from the north in August. In September Göring, who by now should have been wary of Dowding's cunning, made one last ploy to tempt the leader of the few to commit all his fighters to the defense of London. But just as Dowding had sacrificed any number of British evacuees at Dunkirk and asked weary, depleted squadrons to fight on against long odds during the summer, so he let entire neighborhoods of the capital be destroyed so that Fighter Command could survive to fight out and eventually win the battle, like the fox who chews his leg free of the trap and limps away, while the hunter's bag remains empty.

In the air the fighter style was to range freely, even though organized tactics often dictated otherwise. Pilots always had a ready

73

answer to justify their sometimes renegade quests for freedom, but a more likely explanation is a deep-seated reluctance to take orders once airborne. Douglas Bader felt this way, arguing that the "chap in the air" and not the controller on the ground should have the final say about undertaking an aerial engagement. Don Bennett, who became famous as leader of the Pathfinder target-marking force, pleaded throughout his career in both civil and military aviation that no airborne pilot should have to accept any order from ground personnel, and he could rattle off a series of botched instructions that had sent innocent, dutiful airmen to their deaths. Although ground-controlled interception was the keystone of British defense and maximized RAF effectiveness in the Battle of Britain, individual pilots were forever breaking off on their own sweeps; Johnnie Johnson reports Douglas Bader approaching another pilot on an air test and suggesting that "You and I will slide up through this bit of cloud, nip across the Channel and see if we can bag a couple of Huns before lunch. It will be a pleasant surprise for Flight Lieutenant Holden" (p. 62).

German pilots felt the same way, and in *The First and the Last* Adolf Galland argues the merits of fighter freedom directly to Herman Göring, who has insisted Galland's units fly close cover for the bombers being savaged by RAF attacks:

> Obviously the proximity and the visible presence of the protective fighters gave the bomber pilots a greater sense of security. However, this was a faulty conclusion, because a fighter can only carry out this purely defensive task by taking the initiative in the offensive. He must never wait until he is attacked because he then loses the chance of acting. The fighter must seek battle in the air, must find his opponent, attack him, and shoot him down. The bomber must avoid such fights and he has to act defensively, in order to fulfill his task: war from the air. In cooperation between bomber and fighter, these two fundamentally different mentalities obviously clashed. The words of Richthofen expressed during World War I, summarizing the task of the fighters, often came to our lips. Fundamentally they are still valid today. "The fighter pilots have to rove in the area allotted to them in any way they like, and when they spot an enemy they attack and shoot him down; anything else is rubbish." (p. 32)

The universality of these tactics is shown in *Nine Lives,* when Wing Leader Al Deere flatly refuses to let a squadron of B-26 Marauders even think about requesting close formation support. For his wing's aggressive sweeps Deere plans a strategy giving each of his three squadrons a new independence emphasizing mutual support rather than mass control, and the results are gratifying. As wing leader he sets the routes and timings, leaving the individual squadron leaders "free to act on their own initiative to engage enemy aircraft on sighting, first warning me that they intend to break formation" (Deere, p. 229). To Deere's plan Douglas Bader, a wing leader himself, adds a further dose of independence by freeing his larger wings from close ground control. He argues that his forces need the latitude to engage the enemy, as Len Deighton notes in *Fighter*, "at the time, the place, and in the fashion that the formation leader saw fit" (p. 230).

Independence is so close to the fighter pilot's heart that years afterward he will yearn for battles that never took place, for engagements that would have made history had the controllers allowed them to happen. Adolf Galland regrets especially the combat formations ordered for Luftwaffe fighters in the last year of the war, which teamed fighters and Messerschmitt 110 destroyers in concentrated but unwieldy masses to provide both offense against American heavy bombers and defense against their P-51 Mustang escorts. This tactic, however, means "renouncing the fundamental principle of all fighter action" (p. 249), which is free offense. It now becomes much easier for the Americans to organize their defense, frustrating Galland's desire for one-to-one combat. "Only in this way," he concludes sadly, "can it be explained that the great struggle for air supremacy over Germany between the opposing fighters never took place" (p. 250).

What then is the fighter style? According to Galland it includes "aggressive spirit, joy of action, and the passion of the hunter. The fighter arm cannot be manacled, particularly when its fetters are determined by earth-bound thinking. By its intrinsic properties the fighter arm belongs to the elite" (p. 66). When this style is frustrated, fighters are relegated to the status of a "fire brigade," their strength "frittered away" by the "dictatorship of ground ideas" (p. 80). Galland sees this happening more and more in the Luftwaffe and less and less in the American air forces, which, after the German aircraft industry is destroyed, are allowed to abandon their defensive role and "go over to the offensive," at which time the "superiority of the American fighter [came] into its own" (p. 264). With this theory and practice in mind it is easy to appreciate the joy Bob Braham expresses in *"Scramble!"* when his squadron is "given a remarkably free hand" (p. 133) by bypassing the control elements of Sector and Group (Bader's dream!) and reporting directly to Fighter Command for guidance in its intruder role among the bomber stream over Germany. Ranging freely among the RAF heavy bombers, Braham's Beaufighters seek out German night fighters, occasionally shooting them down and always confusing the air defenses and worrying the night fighter crews into a state of ineffectiveness. Within the bomber stream the Beaufighters remain undetected, while their freedom of offensive movement lets them dart in and out at will as targets of opportunity present themselves. A sounder demonstration of Galland's theory of free offense cannot be found.

Because the Luftwaffe was developed ahead of the RAF, converting to high-speed monoplanes several years before the British and testing their new equipment under fire in Spain, the German pilots had the advantage of bringing pertinent new fighter tactics into the war, whereas their RAF counterparts had to learn—often painfully—from their example. As a lieutenant in Spain, the future General of Fighters Werner Mölders devised a combat formation opposite in every respect to RAF squadron practice, and in the early days of the Battle of Britain Luftwaffe fighter pilots used it with great success, as Dennis Knight describes in *Harvest of Messerschmitts:*

> At this time [July 1940] the RAF used fighters in combinations of three, a section leader and two wingmen. A full squadron consisted of four sections—usually called Red, Blue, Yellow and Green—all twelve aircraft keeping in an orderly tight formation, with two rear machines weaving so as to watch the sky above and behind. Invariably, the novice pilots got the job of weaving and, time and again, British squadrons were bounced by enterprising Messerschmitt pilots, who would dive in pairs very quickly, fire and disengage. One would be the marksman and hunter, the other his No. 2 guarding his rear.
>
> Mölders advocated that two such pairs made an ideal combat formation when flying loosely in what was called a "Schwarm." In an engagement, the "Schwarm" endeavored to stay together, but, if necessary, it broke down into pairs: a lone fighter was ineffectual and vulnerable. When a formation turned, the inside pairs crossed over those on the outside so as to reverse positions, completing the manoeuvre quickly and not having the problem of speed differentials on the inside and outside, as experienced by British formations during a turn. (p. 83)

To Mölder's "Schwarm" Adolf Galland added the refinements of greater intervals within the smaller formations and between the larger groups, so that the "first rule of combat," that of seeing the opponent first, could be better implemented (p. 25). The outmoded RAF tactic of entering combat in line-astern formation took away just this advantage, for so much of the pilot's attention went to keeping in close formation that large areas of the sky remained unwatched. RAF fliers quickly saw the advantages of the "Schwarm" and renamed it the "finger four," employing it to great effect by having the first wingman fly to the leader's sun side and low (so that he could guard against out-of-the-sun attacks while still letting his comrades see him), the second wingman taking the same position but a bit higher to spot planes approaching from above. With all four aircraft at different altitudes, the loose formation could be held with less bother while covering all four quarters of the sky.

Line-astern attacks had been written into the book during the mid 1930s, when air force tacticians theorized that the high speed of emerging fighter designs would obviate any chances for World War I–style dogfighting. The experiences of summer 1940 proved differently, and soon the RAF's best pilots were looking back to the first war for inspiration and technique. In *Reach for the Sky* Paul Brickhill describes Douglas Bader arguing with his senior squadron members, most of whom still hold to the theory of strict formation attacks:

> "The chap who'll control the battle will still be the chap who's got the height and the sun, same as the last war," he said. "That old slogan of Ball, Bishop and McCudden, 'Beware of the Hun in the sun,' wasn't just a funny rhyme. Those boys learned from experience. We haven't got the experience yet, so I'll back their ideas till I find out." (p. 160)

Bader's latter-day German adversaries had already reintroduced just such tactics themselves, and by the time a younger man like Richard Hillary could complete his training (from veterans of the Battle of France), the lessons of Luftwaffe performance were clear. "We learned of the advantage of height and of attacking out of the sun," Hillary recounts; "of the German's willingness to fight with height and odds in their favor and their disinclination to mix it on less favorable terms" (p. 61).

With the finger four adopted, RAF fighters were now able to face the Luftwaffe on at least tactically even terms. Had the squadrons stuck to their old procedures, it is doubtful Fighter Command would have survived the Battle of Britain, for added to the

Luftwaffe's greater numbers the specific disadvantages of the old formations would have been an insurmountable obstacle. Now, instead of vulnerable tail-end Charlie waiting to be picked off from a line-astern formation, each member of the finger four, in Johnnie Johnson's words, "is well up with his colleagues and stands an equal chance of survival" (p. 38). Both the line-astern and vic-three formations had made the major task of flying that of keeping in proper order; now effort could be better spent on watching for the enemy. Visibility above and aside was improved, but not as greatly as visibility below. The wings of a Spitfire, when flown at its normal operational height of twenty-five thousand feet, hide over a thousand square miles of area below, but the greater maneuverability of the finger four and the greater distances between planes (about two hundred yards instead of wingtip to wingtip) allowed a greater range of vision and of action. It was an easier formation to fly and lent itself to immediate breakdown into efficient fighting units of two planes, the *Rotte* the German Condor Legion used so well in Spain.

Adopting the finger four was a natural move—Paul Brickhill describes how Bader's and Johnson's Tangmere squadron worked out its tactics in less than a week—and in practice its results were gratifying: the two aircraft broke off together when under attack in order to maintain the tandem duties of a leader to shoot and a wingman to guard him. Turning on the outside, the leader's wingman retains his height advantage as the two other Spitfires slip inside his number one, all within sight of each other to maintain cross cover against marauding Messerschmitts. Again, these were tactics worked out by individual squadrons during Battle of Britain sorties previous to their incorporation within training. Since the typical Luftwaffe fighter pilot timed his diving attack in mere seconds, there was no time for elaborate maneuvers—RAF reaction had to be simple and quick. All of the fancy aerobatics, learned with such diligence and practiced with such joy, were meant simply to give pilots confidence in their machines.

Other rules of combat soon became obvious. Douglas McRoberts lists them in *Lions Rampant,* drawing comparisons with similar rules in World War I: "Never fly in a straight line for more than two seconds in combat. The pilot who has the height advantage controls the battle. Never follow your victim down—the chances are his wing man will nail you. Above all, 'Beware the Hun in the sun!' " (p. 71). The optimum burst of fire is two seconds; any longer severely retards one's airspeed, already reduced forty miles per hour by the guns' recoil, which makes one an easy and inviting target for the Messerschmitt behind. This is just how Richard Hillary gets shot down, and he recognizes his mistake the moment it happens:

> I closed in to 200 yards and from slightly one side gave him a two-second burst; fabric ripped off the wing and black smoke poured from the engine, but he did not go down. Like a fool, I did not break away, but put in another three-second burst. Red flames shot upwards and he spiralled out of sight. At that moment I felt a terrific explosion which knocked the control stick from my hand, and the whole machine quivered like a stricken animal. In a second, the cockpit was a mass of flames. (p. 7)

Bomber pursuit proves to be a game of quickness, just like dogfighting. Here prewar tactics are even more ridiculously at odds with the realities of speed and armament. In *The Luck of the Devil* A. E. "Tony" Dudgeon has fun with the "lunacy" of the Manual of Air Combat, which describes a training exercise far removed from what any fighter pilot might hope to encounter in an attack:

> First, one aeroplane would fly, in broad daylight, at a reduced speed, straight and level at 10,000 feet. This was "The Bomber." The flight of three fighters would approach from behind in close formation and pretend to fire their single, fixed, forward-firing machine guns. Then the flight would turn away. This completed Exercise 1. In real life, if the idiot bomber held still long enough, the attacking leader might fire. For his wingmen it would be impossible because you cannot hold your aircraft in the formation position, and at the same time point it at an enemy. The one contradicts the other. But no matter; that was what was written in the good book. In any case the question was academic since we had no forward-mounted camera-guns to prove the point. (p. 54)

Bob Braham, practicing the same exercise against target bombers, complains that "the attacks laid down in the tactics manual were of little value, as most of the time we were sitting ducks for the rear gunner of the Wellingtons, Hampdens and Whitleys" (p. 37). What is needed is either patient, individual, and above all secretive stalking from a gunner's blind spot or a swift diving attack. Once the enemy is engaged, the shooting should take but a few seconds, as Squadron Leader Archie McKellar demonstrates over Maidstone when he faces a group of German bombers head on:

The gap closed at a frightening rate, but McKellar's Hurricane was rock-steady. Throttling back, to increase his firing time fractionally, he flew straight for the Heinkel leader in a slight dive. At 500 yards his guns flashed; the Heinkel shuddered, its perspex nose shattered into a thousand fragments, its leading edges taking fire. Archie saw a glow within the fuselage, and he swerved, "walking" his fire onto the bomber on the leader's left. Simultaneously, three things happened. The left-hand bomber, Archie's second target, lost a wing, severed at the root; the center machine exploded, clearly with its bombs still on board; and the right-hand machine burst into flames, turned on its back and dived uncontrollably earthwards. With a single four-second burst of fire, he had destroyed three twin-engined bombers. Seconds after opening fire, Archie flew through the patch of sky which had contained the Luftwaffe machines. There were only a few scraps of debris to impede his progress. (McRoberts, p. 124)

Since these tactics were devised after most of the Battle of Britain pilots were trained, learning them became an important on-the-job task. Because of their prior experience in Spain, Poland, and France, and thanks to their aggressive posture in the fray with Great Britain, the Luftwaffe pilots were good, if involuntary, teachers. It was the Messerschmitt *Jagdstaffel* that provided the example of how well a four-man unit working in pairs could both attack and defend. Flying convoy patrol, Al Deere's squadron dives upon a dozen Messerschmitt 109s, which surprise him with a new tactical refinement: one group breaks upward and to the right in a steep turn, while the other also breaks upward but to the left. "No fool this leader" (p. 89), Deere says to himself; he notes the smart move and resolves to use it if his own squadron is ever jumped in similar circumstances. The time to use it does come, much later in the war, when the predators are the dangerous Focke-Wulf 190s, but Deere has practiced the maneuver for years and it now works perfectly against its inventors.

All British veterans, however, are not such good teachers as the Luftwaffe. In his own memoir Johnnie Johnson complains of his instructors at Hawarden, "most of whom had fought in France, over Dunkirk or in the preliminary phases of the Battle of Britain," who "rarely spoke to the pupils of their combats against the Messerschmitts." No lectures on combat tactics had yet been devised, and with nothing in the book, nothing was taught. Johnson's fellow students were eager to ask questions: How did squadrons fight squadrons and wings take on wings? What about the Messerschmitt 109's

new propeller-hub cannon and turning radius? Was it better to concentrate on shooting or on following the leader? "All these and a
hundred questions remained unanswered," Johnson laments, "for the
handful of instructors hung together and had their work cut out to
keep the sausage machine turning" (pp. 16–17). Their motives are not
as cruel as those of the operational instructors Keith Park encoun-
tered in World War I. As Park's biographer, Vincent Orange, reveals,
these flight commanders told new pilots nothing and led them into
battle to be sacrificed as "good bait" (p. 19) for the attacking Germans, who, after making their tantalizingly easy kills, fell victim to
the Royal Air Service veterans. But the same independence that
prompted fighter pilots to devise their own tactics and refit their own
machines dissuaded them from relying too much on their fellow fliers.
Tony Dudgeon, whose RAF career spanned several decades, puts the
matter in perspective:

> I suppose that the remarkable lack of outside aids to the
> early pilot was, if anything, the factor that built up an independ-
> ence of spirit with moral and physical courage, initiative and
> oomph that enabled us to win World War II—well, if not the
> whole war, great chunks of it like the Battle of Britain. Once you
> were airborne in an early craft you were on your own. No one
> could guide you, help you or advise you—or tell you not to do
> something dangerous. Perhaps this explains why so many of us
> killed ourselves through "pilot error." The excitement of flying,
> backed by a devil-may-care personality, is a great mixture for
> war—if you survive to reach it. Slowly, all too slowly, I was to
> learn that my machine was simply a superb servant—and a stag-
> geringly dangerous toy. (p. 5)

Added to the newly evolved tactics were the fighter pilot's skills,
some of which were natural, while others had to be learned. Buzz
Beurling, the outlaw hero of Malta, was renowned for his superb
shooting, which many considered a lucky gift. His biographer, Brian
Nolan, however, emphasizes that "Beurling refuted any suggestion
that it was a natural ability, insisting that it was an acquired skill, one
which he pursued with dogged determination" (p. 53). Combat flying
did allow the option of a straight shot, but it was by far the most
dangerous, leaving the attacker himself open to predators. Slow stalking from the rear was possible against bombers at night, but successful day fighting, especially against Messerschmitts and Focke-Wulfs,
depended on how quickly a Spitfire or Hurricane pilot could get off

his first shot after spotting the enemy. This meant firing at an angle —
"deflection shooting," as it came to be called — and involved instantaneous estimates of relative speed and a knowledge of solid geometry.
To perfect the technical side of these skills, the pilot must make his
own study, as Nolan details:

> As soon as Beurling arrived on Malta, he began recording
> the details of each of his successful attacks and each of his misses
> in a black book. He then designed a set of formulae and a graph
> that took into account the thousands of pieces of information he
> had compiled. The formulae and the graphs were then committed
> to memory so that, when the occasion arose, he could draw on
> this information in a split second, an Olympian feat of mental
> gymnastics that could have been performed only by a brilliant
> natural mathematician. (p. 55)

At play Beurling shows the same dedication, potting lizards at the
relative distance it would take for the reptile to represent an enemy
fighter at three hundred yards. Back in England he alienates his fellow pilots by shooting the tail feather off a pet wood duck, but even in
repose the notorious hero of Malta declines Johnnie Johnson's offer
to come in for a late-night beer with the excuse, "No thanks, Wingco.
Guess I'll stay out here. I'm figuring the angles between the stars"
(Johnson, p. 167).

Heading into combat, the fighter pilot sports a dashing style.
Even the legless Bader acts as if "immune from nerves, a rollicking
figure in black flying suit and blue and white polka-dot silk scarf,
stuffing his pipe into his pocket when he hoisted himself into the
cockpit" (Brickhill, *Reach for the Sky,* p. 261). Combat comes
quickly; Pierre Closterman is always surprised by how suddenly a
Messerschmitt 109 or Focke-Wulf 190 can appear. Rarely are the metaphors that describe these engagements banal — plane and pilot are
commonly compared to a well-coordinated horse and rider — but more
often the literal details of dogfighting are adequate to produce a lively
narrative. A favorite moment in *The Big Show* is when an enemy
aircraft sweeps close enough for Closterman to see the pilot's face,
although it is often blurred and occasionally disfigured by helmet and
goggles so as to resemble "some queer insect" (p. 41); such episodes
are most impressive when the human reactions of doubt or fear show
through. Closterman's narrative constantly oscillates between fact
and fantasy, as the rigors of battle play havoc with his perception,
yielding a contest of sensations in his mind: "I had the impression I

was diving into an aquarium of demented fish! Nothing but radial engines, yellow bellies, black crosses, and clipped wings beating the air like fins. The air was criss-crossed with multi-colored tracer bullets, and instinctively I blinked" (p. 62). Closterman's best similes are based on the sharp observation of color and thus are closely anchored in the situation of combat; a Messerschmitt 109G "shone like a newly-minted penny" (p. 86) [in the French he refers to a *centime,* a coin quite yellow in color]; he describes any number of German planes whose yellow noses, pale grey upper surfaces, and sky-blue undersides create the image of an Impressionist's swirling palette.

There are tricks to combat, and some of the best of them are improvised or recalled in utterly hopeless predicaments. With four Mustangs on his tail, Adolf Galland is a sure victim until he tries an old Battle of Britain trick that had saved his life twice before: "I fired everything I had simply into the blue in front of me. It had the desired effect on my pursuers. Suddenly they saw the smoke which the shells had left behind coming toward them. They probably thought they had met the first fighter to fire backward or that a second attacking German fighter arm was behind them" (p. 254). The American planes break away and disappear, and Galland once again survives. Other pilots fight with more abandon and even with recklessness, but always for a reason. Johnnie Johnson writes of a colleague who flies with no regard for himself or for the mechanical condition of his Hurricane; with sympathy for neither himself or his enemy, he once destroys a bomber at such close range that pieces of human flesh and blood stain his aircraft, which he refuses to have cleaned. The reason? "We heard that his wife and children had been killed in one of the Manchester blitzes, and it was said that he screamed, like a man demented, at the sight of the enemy bombers" (p. 57). In the happier parts of *Wing Leader* Johnson praises the conscientious skill of pilots like the one who escapes a pair of pursuing Messerschmitt 109s over France by making it seem he will crash:

> This time he foxed them by half-rolling his Spitfire and holding it, inverted, in a shallow dive. The 109s drew off to watch the end, but our pilot had seen a reasonable field and as he crossed the boundary hedge he rolled back to a normal attitude and smacked the Spitfire into an excellent wheels-up landing. He stepped out of the wreck unscathed, with the 109s still milling overhead. This remarkable character later returned on foot via Spain and Gibraltar. (p. 81)

The climax of an attack or dogfight is the moment when the enemy is shot down, and every memoir is distinguished by the vivid writing occasioned by these scenes. Sometimes the moment is coolly premeditated, as when in *Night Fighter* Rawnsley and his pilot Cunningham fly along in company with a Heinkel for three or four minutes "while we calmly decided on the fate of the four men above us. It was all quite leisurely and well ordered and not at all what I had anticipated it would be like" (p. 85). Adolf Galland experiences the same sensation when, after having peppered a Hurricane with repeated fire, he "flew close alongside the flying wreck, by now thoroughly riddled, with smoke belching from her. From a distance of a few yards I saw the dead pilot sitting in his shattered cockpit, while his aircraft spiraled slowly to the ground as though piloted by a ghostly hand" (p. 44).

The crash of an enemy aircraft is a delicate matter for memoirists on both sides, for although an air combat is surely to the death, few fliers relish personally destroying the human being within the plane. As a result, their narratives shift from notes on blurred faces and the human characteristics of their planes in combat to a technological description of the crash. In *Spitfire Command* Bobby Oxspring describes shooting down a Messerschmitt 109 north of Folkestone. He records the pilot bailing out but gives more space at this point to a postwar comparison of notes with his adversary of forty years before, Leutnant Erich Bodendiek. The page is filled with technical commentary on the German flier's troubles with his experimental variable-pitch propeller: "This restricted his speed particularly in the climb, and he was unable to reach the cover of the high cirrus as the others of his flight had done when we attacked" (p. 77). Later, when the ignoring of Oxspring's early warning about the developing breakout of the German capital ships *Scharnhorst, Gneisenau,* and *Prinz Eugen* leads to the loss of a tardily attacking Swordfish squadron, Oxspring textualizes the experience by comparing his own notes with the enemy account in Adolf Galland's *The First and the Last* and thus sparing his narrative the trauma of recrimination.

The one glaring exception to such delicate dealings is Buzz Beurling's oft-told story of blowing the head off an Italian pilot in an open-cockpit fighter. In all other cases the enemy planes are shot down dispassionately, as if they had no crew at all (where people are mentioned, as in Galland's and Rawnsley's attacks, details of the crash are omitted). Pierre Closterman's kill of a Focke-Wulf 190 at low altitude over France sets the style of description, which is paced by the frantic hedge hopping and quick depletion of ammunition.

> But I had got him! At appalling speed the Focke-Wulf, still on its back, hit the ground and slid, scattering incandescent fragments everywhere, leaving a trail of blazing fuel, hurtled through two hedges and crashed against a road bank in a dazzling shower of sparks.
>
> Fascinated, I only pulled out in the nick of time to avoid a row of telegraph poles. Climbing up in spirals at full throttle I cast a look down. The petrol-sodden grass formed a fiery crown round the charred skeleton of the Focke-Wulf and the oily smoke swept by the wind drifted heavily towards the village of Hazebrouck. (p. 42)

The episode's only personal pronoun is expended quickly at the start. Its disappearance transfers attention from pilot to machine for the remainder of the description; from here on only the Focke-Wulf is mentioned, never its Luftwaffe pilot. The plane itself is suddenly transmogrified into the elements of fire and light, as is all of nature around it, even the grass and the wind. The single term that implies a human body—"skeleton"—startles us for a moment, but is quickly applied to the plane's airframe, not to its unfortunate occupant, though there is surely a charred human body within it. Closterman leaves that idea to our imagination, after nearly being consumed by the conflagration himself. Deep thinkers of the world, beware: air combat is no time or place for thoughts of the humanly real.

The scene of destruction is even more compelling at night, when a stricken aircraft blazes all the more brightly as it falls. When Cunningham and Rawnsley bring down a Heinkel, even strictly empirical language is fraught with extremes of color and light:

> John fired only forty rounds, straight into the fuselage. There was a flash and some smoke, and pieces came flying back over us. The metal of the skin of the Heinkel began to burn as it sank into a long, shallow dive, and the trail it left, white and molten, caught the eyes of the searchlight crews. Triumphantly the beams held the wretched bomber until it shone like silver in the cone of a dozen lights. It dived out of sight beneath us, still dripping white fire, as though melting in the intensity of the searchlight beams. (Rawnsley, p. 126)

How can an airplane be "wretched"? In the same way that it can "drip white fire" within the light of "triumphant" searchlights. In Rawnsley's description all animation has been displaced from the human operators to their machines, which then suffer the consequences of aerial destruction. When another bomber crashes a few minutes later, Rawnsley admits to being horrified when its blazing red glow reveals walls and windows in the surrounding neighborhood; he is relieved when he sees that it is an abandoned, bombed-out area, cleared of people whose corpses would ethically distort the precision of his language.

Most times the kill is made at a distance great enough to let all human consequences disappear behind a mask of technology. When cannons shatter perspex hoods at three hundred yards, the attacking pilot is more aware of a shattering of crystal slivers than the destruction of a man behind that glass. Even when John Cunningham eases their Beaufighter close behind a fighter-bomber to confirm its identity, Rawnsley is startled not by his proximity to the enemy airmen inside but by the "great dirty bomb" slung beneath its fuselage (p. 273).

Distance becomes an ally when the crash observed is not of an enemy but of a friend. High above the English Channel on night interception duty, Rawnsley can see far into Germany and watch "the inferno of shell fire going up from the Ruhr" when it is attacked. He can also watch crippled British bombers plummet; from two hundred fifty miles away they appear as "fireballs" (p. 269). The tendency to depersonalize a crash persists even when the observer is nearby, as John Golley, in *The Day of the Typhoon,* and Pierre Closterman, in *The Big Show,* reveal when the tactical fighter-bombers they are escorting disappear in the smoke of a bomb explosion and leave no trace of themselves within its crater. Escorting heavy bombers often prompts effusive admiration of their huge formations, but only as a preliminary to pitying their ragged holes upon return—in each case a matter of aesthetic form rather than human sympathy.

When in the fall of 1940 the Luftwaffe shifts to mostly night attacks, the fighter style faces a complex challenge. The aircraft which had performed so well during the Battle of Britain were not designed as night fighters. Both the Spitfire and the Hurricane destroyed their pilots' night vision with bright exhaust flames. On the Hurricane these flames could be damped, but the structure of daytime combat— single-seat fighters flying together in pairs, sections, squadrons, and wings — was not suitable for night combat, as Johnnie Johnson explains:

> We never became proficient in this type of work, largely because the requirement itself was a basic contradiction of all our training. During the day we fought and lived like a team, and this was the very essence of our squadron and wing formation. When we climbed our Spitfires into the darkness we were oppressed not only by the strange loneliness of our solitary flights but by the thought of our own severe limitations in the task ahead. (p. 57)

The most common beginning for any night fighter narrative is this sense of isolation, a feeling Peter Townsend, in *Duel in the Dark,* finds almost overwhelming, as he sits alone in his Hurricane with no effective communication except the flame of his exhausts, which though now shielded from his eyes can be seen for hundreds of miles by the enemy bombers he hopes to stalk. At least the Hurricane boasts a large cockpit and a wide, rugged undercarriage to ease the night landings, so that for the first season of night attacks the RAF is able to mount at least a token defense, though the number of German intruders brought down is small.

The answer to the night fighter problem is twofold: an aircraft specially designed for the purpose — the Beaufighter — and a two-man crew of pilot and radar observer working closely as a team. As an intermediate step the Blenheim's dorsal turret is removed and its gunner retrained as an Air Interception operator. One of the first of these AI men is C. F. Rawnsley, who is teamed with the leading night fighter pilot, John Cunningham. Their exploits extend from the early years of experiment and frustration to the period of expertise enjoyed as the war drew to a close. Unlike the exhilarating day combat narratives, Rawnsley's *Night Fighter* is a tale of constant struggle: the challenge of fighting in the dark, the improvised conditions aboard the Blenheim, the balkiness of early AI equipment and its intricacies of operation, the close cooperation demanded between operator and pilot, the ambiguous status of operators (were they entitled to wear the air badge?), the challenge of adapting to the new Beaufighter and its more complex equipment, the demoralizing odds at which these fliers fought while London burned, and even "the relentless and ever-present law of gravity," a foe so familiar and implacable that it earned the name "Sir Isaac Newton" (p. 25). From start to finish Rawnsley faces a personal challenge not evident in the day fighter memoirs: an occasional lack of confidence in his own skills, which even repeated success cannot resolve, since the "black magic" of their weird equipment and the conditions in which they fly dictate that they are always "working in the dark, in almost every way" (p. 42). The brilliance of their kills cannot be acknowledged publicly, for the radar equipment and Rawnsley's operation of it are top secret; instead, the public is told that Cunningham's success is due to his "cat's eyes" talent for seeing in the dark.

Certain night interceptions are more important than others, such as bagging a plane on target indicator duty, the equivalent of an RAF Pathfinder known in the Luftwaffe as a "fire lighter," which pays double dividends if shot down before it can accomplish its task of marking the target for succeeding bombers. The interception of enemy aircraft at night is a more cautious affair than during the day, for making a positive identification in the dark is a long and difficult task. Cunningham's practice is to stalk his victim from just below its tail. If he cannot identify the plane from this blind spot, he then pulls almost vertically below the aircraft, from which point its silhouette stands out as clearly as on a recognition chart. Once he is sure of his target, he pulls up in a firing position just below and behind to let the German bomber have it. "On no account," Rawnsley cautions, "must there be, for John, any rushing in with hit-or-miss tactics" (p. 77). Thus, the pace of night fighting is just the opposite of that of day fighting. Rather than quick spotting and instantaneous attack—the two rules Bader, Johnson, and the other day fighters mastered—Rawnsley and Cunningham are pledged to hours of patient patrolling, which lead, when successful, to a slow stalking of the target, like a hunter creeping through the woods.

Viewing the battle through his AI scope presents quite an odd picture to Rawnsley. Instead of the yellow-nosed, blue-bellied fighters of Closterman's narrative and the ugly black Heinkels Peter Townsend shoots down on daytime duty in the war's first year, Rawnsley's adversaries are blips on a green cathode ray tube. The equipment is mystical and mystifying, and occasionally produces startling results, as when a target suddenly breaks in half and one part hurtles to the ground—which part a moment later Rawnsley realizes is the plane's bomb load. But as the "boffins" bring forth better technology from their labs, the operators are quick to adapt it to their own expertise, as happens when a new style of AI set allows observers to scan backward as well as forward:

Some of the more agile and adventurous radar equipped intruder crews soon developed a system of tactics whereby they even allowed themselves to be intercepted, waiting for the attacker to move in, more or less dangling them on their invisible radar string. And then, with a very nice timing and a vigorous use of their aircraft, they would whip right around on the tail of the other aircraft and quickly complete an interception of their own. (Rawnsley, p. 253)

Physically, an entirely different battle is taking place, both inside the aircraft, as the AI operator struggles with his strange equipment, and outside, as the air defenses turn the night sky into an inferno. Guiding his Junkers 88 over The Wash in a raid on Liverpool, Luftwaffe pilot Peter Stahl is caught by the searchlights and finds the experience surreal:

It is like flying through an endless tunnel of light. After a while we note furious AA [antiaircraft] fire to port and starboard coming up from the areas around Nottingham/Derby and Sheffield/Manchester, but apart from this never-before-experienced effort by searchlights, everything is quiet around us. This quiet is really uncanny. I try every trick I know to mislead them down there, but in vain. Every time I change my direction, the searchlights just follow me. Even the usually effective method of deceiving the defenses, by changing the revs of the engines to alter their sound, fails this time. We are captured and delivered! It is obvious we have landed on a strip in the sky reserved for night fighters, these fellows we dread most of all, because their tactics, in contrast to the AA guns, are "silent" and unseen. In a situation like this, one feels completely offered up without any possibility of defending oneself, either by superior flying skill or the use of one's armament. Whoever sees the other first is the winner. We know this only too well, and literally stare our eyes out of our heads. (pp. 133–35)

At this point in the war, the Germans are still unaware of the RAF's top-secret radar, but Stahl's anxiously roving glance complements Rawnsley's when he looks from his AI set out onto the scene below:

The raid was in full swing as we turned back towards base, and for once I was free to get a good view of what was happening outside. So much of my time had been spent gazing at those cathode ray tubes; and what I saw now was an awe-inspiring sight. All along the way from Dungeness to London there was a constantly moving carpet of searchlights. It was almost as if they were bearing the visitors aloft from box to box on the apex of their cones.

The enemy pathfinders had already carpeted the route with a great series of oval splashes of white markers, turning the seventy tormented miles of Bomb Alley into a dazzling Great White Way. At the end of that floodlit highway the inferno of the London barrage twinkled and flickered above a criss-cross pattern of spouting tracer and rocket salvoes that seemed to split the heavens.

And along its length, on a front ten miles wide and five miles deep, the airborne traffic ran the gauntlet. Fifty or sixty aircraft, for the most part unseen, hurtled along as fast as overspeeding engines could carry them, twisting and diving, their crews either staring out at the waving beams of the searchlights or crouching over their radar sets, watching with agonized intentness those insignificant looking little blips on the cathode ray tubes whose movements meant success or failure, life or death, to the watchers. (Rawnsley, p. 320)

Within this eerie spectacle a close relationship between pilot and crew is mandatory. Stahl writes of the kinship he feels with his three colleagues in the Junkers bomber, and Rawnsley's *Night Fighter* is as much a testament to Cunningham's skill as to his own. Indeed, there is an almost uxorial feeling between the AI operator and his pilot. Bob Braham remarks in *"Scramble!"* that he is "wedded" (p. 60) to his observer, and Rawnsley often acts as timid and insecure as a new bride fearful of disappointing her husband in some duty. The night fighter pilots who achieved ace status were few, but all were quick to credit the expertise of their AI operators, without whose electronic eyes the Beaufighter would be flying blind, with no better chance at making an interception than Johnson's and Townsend's forlorn Spitfires and Hurricanes in the bleak early days. Rawnsley makes a psychological case for honesty, reasoning that the conditions of nighttime air interception could easily breed suspicion and self-deception and that there would have to be "a truthful and mutual understanding between the pilot and the operator" (p. 71) for problems to be resolved, given how easy it was for one to blame the other within the privacy of his vision. Better to appreciate the particular difficulty of each other's work, which is the understanding Cunningham and Rawnsley achieve. Braham acknowledges the secret, which works with his own operator: "complete co-ordination and implicit faith in each other" (p. 71).

"Scramble!" and *Night Fighter* make interesting narrative comparisons. One is written by a pilot, the other by an AI operator, yet each pertains to the extremely circumscribed world of night interception, an arena that allows far less individuality than the day combats celebrated by Johnson, Bader, Closterman, and Hillary. On key issues Braham and Rawnsley agree, particularly about the new Mark 5 equipment, which provides a scope for the pilot as well as for the AI man. Rawnsley complains about it at length, for it threatens his own role and the spirit of cooperation. In truth, however, he has little to fear, for Cunningham continues to trust his operator and Braham objects that it is too difficult to refocus his eyes from scope to live target. The pilot's scope remains in the Beaufighter, but it is largely ignored.

Metaphors of night combat are sometimes more creative than their daytime counterparts, for as opposed to the abundance of visual imagery in the dogfights over England, the Channel, and France, darkness generally provides a blank screen on which to project one's imagination. Rawnsley takes special delight in such invention; he thinks of the ground controller as a friendly barman taking orders for drinks and his pilot as a lift operator, easing his Beaufighter behind a bomber for the attack. During these stalkings Rawnsley is often "seized with a ridiculous feeling of a need for stealth, and I wanted to talk in whispers, to peer cautiously around corners, to move on tiptoe" as the target looms ahead (p. 93). Another time he thinks of his plane as a submarine, just at periscope depth, shadowing an enemy ship.

The narrative plot of most British night fighter stories is that of a slow and often painful progress from failure to success, with an alternating tone of frustration and elation marking the way. German memoirs are much different, partly because of the rising action toward a losing cause as more and more bombers fly over Germany, but also because of tactical limitations most writers lament. Wilhelm Johnen, in *Duel Under the Stars,* while mostly an action narrative, makes frequent pauses to criticize the way his plane is tied so tightly to sector control and hence unable to accommodate the frequent RAF feints and diversions. Adolf Galland's *The First and the Last* is more consistently devoted to discussions of theory, during which he complains that Luftwaffe night forces are improperly and hastily trained and are not allowed the range necessary to follow bombers to and from their targets. But his commentary on the last successful style of night combat to be developed reveals the suddenly visual dimension of the war: the "Wild Boar" method of turning loose single-seat, single-engine planes with no electronic interception devices and no guidance from the ground, yet sure of success because of the "huge conflagrations" on the ground, which create "almost daylight conditions" (p. 212).

Day or night, the fighter spirit is strictly an aerial affair. Ground battles are a decidedly demoralizing business for pilots, and it is a sobering experience for Al Deere when, shot down over Belgium during the Dunkirk evacuation, he must struggle for days to retrace a journey which in his Spitfire took less than thirty minutes. Conditions on the ground shock him, and he can understand the infantry's displeasure with the RAF and its sanitized version of glory. When the air war shifts to the offensive, few pilots enjoy the new types of attack, despite their colorful names. In a "Circus" as many as two hundred fighters escort a small group of bombers used to lure the enemy into the air; air combat must be undertaken with the bait's protection in mind and therefore is nothing like the Battle of Britain's fighting. "Rodeo" is the code name for a large-scale fighter sweep without bombers, a ploy which rarely draws the Luftwaffe since the odds would be unfavorable. "Ramrod" signifies conventional bomber escort, "Roadstead" an attack on coastal shipping. Most infamous is the "Rhubarb," a low-level beat-up by two or four fighters against targets of opportunity such as locomotives, trucks, flak sites, or marshaling yards, almost always undertaken on days when bad weather prevents anything else. RAF displeasure with these tactics is universal, because a high-speed run so close to the ground allows little discrimination in selecting targets, most of which can easily withstand the Spitfire's machine guns, whereas even the smallest caliber ground fire can puncture the plane's glycol tank, which presents a head-on target. Johnnie Johnson's response expresses the feelings of most fliers:

> I loathed those *Rhubarbs* with a deep, dark hatred. Apart from the flak, the hazards of making a let-down over unknown territory and with no accurate knowledge of the cloud base seemed far too great a risk for the damage we inflicted. During the following three summers [1942–44] hundreds of fighter pilots were lost on either small or mass *Rhubarb* operations. Towards the end of 1943, when I finished this tour of ops. and held an appointment of some authority at 11 Group, my strong views on

this subject were given a sympathetic hearing and *Rhubarbs* were discontinued over France, except on very special occasions. (p. 66)

One Rhubarb nets a big catch, if by accident: a section of 602 Squadron prowling outside of Vimoutiers shoots up a Wehrmacht staff car, injuring the great German field marshal, Erwin Rommel. But far more often innocent French civilians die in these raids, and on balance the small gains are hardly to the credit of the RAF.

Apart from its high risk and tactical ambiguity, ground attack leaves an unpleasant taste among pilots on both sides, especially when their guns are effective. In *Duel of Eagles* Peter Townsend deprecates his own work over Dunkirk and records the similar feelings of Luftwaffe pilot Paul Temme. Until this point the enemy was "a *thing,* not a person. They shot at an aircraft with no thought for the men inside it." But with ground strafing the task becomes, in Temme's words, "unadulterated killing. The beaches were jammed full of soldiers. I went up and down at three hundred feet 'hose-piping.' " Townsend agrees that it is "Cold-blooded, point-blank murder. Defenseless men, fathers, sons and brothers, being cruelly massacred by a twenty-four-year-old boy" (p. 238). To attack shipping is no joy for Pierre Closterman, for he sees deck hands being mowed down by his fire, their legs shot out from under them. Even worse are his missions against German armor, especially when he visits the scene of a successful air attack on a Tiger tank, which at first glance appears intact:

> From closer to, however, you could see three small holes — two above one of the tracks and the other plumb in the middle of the black cross painted on the turret, under the long barrel of the 88 mm. gun. Impelled by curiosity Jacques and I went and examined the inside. A shapeless stinking black mass like molten rubber had flowed over the driver's seat and the ammunition boxes and covered the floor. I poked with a stick and a wave of nausea came over me when a shin bone came to light with a few shreds still adhering to it. (p. 114)

The ground, where battles are slow, cumbersome, and gory, is no place for the fighter spirit. The use of fighters and fighter-bombers to close the Falaise pocket in 1944 serves as the climax to this phase of the air war. The carnage is absolutely devastating, the few surviving

Germans shell-shocked and in a state of nervous collapse. Not that many are allowed to survive, as Johnnie Johnson ruefully admits: "Sometimes the retreating enemy waved white sheets at the Spitfires as they hurtled down to attack; but these signs were ignored; our own ground troops were still some distance away and there was no organization available to round up large numbers of prisoners" (p. 237). He calls it one of the great killing grounds of the war and cites General Eisenhower's opinion that the scene could only be described by Dante. "On the last flights," Johnson confirms, "the stench from the decaying bodies below had even penetrated through the cockpit canopies of the Spitfires" (p. 238)—certainly a "poor substitute for the clean, exhilarating thrill of the dog-fight" (p. 239). Even veteran ground attack pilots, like John Golley in *Day of the Typhoon,* are shocked by the carnage at Falaise, where "for the first time in his life" he had come "face to face with the reality of what he was doing" (p. 156). Such warfare demands a different style of aircraft—not the sleek and nimble Spitfire, but the mighty Typhoon, which Golley describes as having "embodied a spirit of aggression with its mighty Sabre engine, cannons and rockets, enormous nose, powerful airframe and vast three-bladed propeller" (p. 207). A Spitfire pilot is happiest when he can stay out of such battles, perhaps to observe from a distance the rare antics of a huge Lancaster strafing the Caen-Falaise road. When a heavy bomber lumbers in to imitate a fighter, the sight is comic. But when fighter pilots have to perform the task themselves, no one can write a happy narrative about it afterward.

Demoralizing as ground attack duties are, one facet of the fighter pilot's life is more debilitating: combat fatigue, or "the twitch." It is inevitably the turning point in the second half of every memoir, including Peter Townsend's *Duel of Eagles.* "I was past caring," Townsend admits near the conclusion. "It was a bad sign; I was more exhausted than I realized" (p. 365). His *Duel in the Dark* ends even more disturbingly, with his body fighting off the barbituates prescribed to calm it. Most pilots resist the fatigue; Pierre Closterman secretly doubles his medical officer's prescription of Benzedrine and acquires the symptoms of drug addiction, including nervous tics and weight loss (seventeen pounds). During the siege of Malta, Buzz Beurling's weight drops from 175 pounds to 140; after an unsuccessful hospitalization it falls to a skeletal 125, and even then he keeps flying. Johnnie Johnson escapes the tell-tale physical signs of fatigue but adopts a sense of reckless aggression and vengeance, which bespeaks the same pressures of long combat:

during this last month I had got into the habit of handing the wing over to a squadron commander and taking my own section down to fight. It was as if the Huns roused a deep personal antagonism in me and a "probable" or a "damaged" did not seem enough. For some reason the enemy aircraft had each to be destroyed, and more than once I found myself at ground-level in single-handed combat with no quarter asked or given. The long tour was beginning to cloud my better judgment. My score stood at twenty-four. (p. 168)

Bob Braham is less fortunate than Johnson, his aggressive spirit and heedlessness of a second attacker bringing him down over Denmark. Night fighting, with its searchlights, flak, and enemy gunners, is an especially hard strain, which creates what Braham admits is a "fatigue which in a perverse sort of way was driving me relentlessly on to take foolish and unnecessary risks in a mad desire to get at the enemy again and again" (p. 182). It is significant that at this point he mentions how the newspapers list him as equal with Johnnie Johnson at twenty-seven kills; though neither man considers it a contest, such publicity adds to the pressure building every day. And so the spectacle continues — Johnson taking more risks, Braham losing caution with his temper, Bader's deep-set eyes darkening with fatigue, Closterman's nerves shattered by flak, and Rawnsley's self-confidence crumbling with every presumed rebuke. The latter's description of what he calls "operational tiredness" is among the best in detailing symptoms of "the twitch":

> I had seen too many others wrestling with it not to recognize the symptoms in myself: the constant weariness, and the carefully concealed relief at finding oneself off duty for the night; the equally carefully feigned eagerness at finding that after all there was a patrol to do . . . . It was not usually any hectic moments in the air that started the thing. I felt that it was more the cumulative, wearing effect of prolonged nervous tension, broken nights, and a very shrewd working knowledge of the law of averages. But it also needed some other factor to trigger the whole thing off: personal problems — including love affairs! — and domestic troubles; some niggling doubt about something or other; or continued failure at the job one was doing. (pp. 194–95)

Nevertheless, pilots and crews push on, resisting all calls for rest. In *The Diving Eagle* Peter Stahl finds that he and his Junkers 88 crew have fallen asleep for hours in mid mission, and in *Squadrons Up!* Noel Monks reports that Hurricane pilots during the Battle of France, flying sorties from 3:14 A.M. to 8:30 P.M., dare not even rest in chairs for fear of lapsing into unrousable sleep. Yet rest tours are hardly that, since pilots are sent to operational training units where instructional tasks are hard and the loss of squadron camaraderie, in Johnson's words, "seemed to resolve itself into a frustrating search to escape. Eventually your stint was over and you went back on ops., far more tired than when you were taken off six months earlier" (p. 106).

The consequences of both combat and fatigue are losses, and it is here the RAF and Luftwaffe narratives, which share the same fighter spirit, diverge. While the British memoirs follow a rising action toward victory, the German memoirs tell a sad story of attrition and mortality. Spitfire pilots seem to have overcome history itself, fighting against overwhelming odds to take back control of the skies above their country and then of Europe itself, reversing the timetable for their destruction. Bader loses his legs but fights back to become the war's most famous flier. On more subtle levels, Braham patches up his battered marriage and Rawnsley overcomes his faltering confidence. In a grand spectacle of triumph over adversity Free French pilots like Pierre Closterman and René Mouchotte struggle back from the loss of virtually everything to become the first members of their RAF squadrons to touch down in June 1944 on the newly won forward airfields in Normandy. Luftwaffe narratives, however, prove unable to transcend the calendar dates of their structure, which lead inexorably to May 8, 1945, the day of the German surrender. Along the way, issues of time and mortality develop in a way unspoken among their British counterparts. As dark as times get in the Battle of Britain, none of the British stories is comparable to Heinz Knoke's entry, in *I Flew for the Führer,* for August 19, 1944:

> There was once a time when I used to count the years of my life by the summers.
> It is different now. This summer is more like a nightmare from which there is no awakening. The heat is oppressive this August in France, as Death reaps his gory harvest: every day I am dodging the strokes of the scythe.
> The worst part of it is the waiting—waiting for the scythe to catch me as it has caught the others, waiting while the hours drag into days, waiting as one day follows inexorably after another. Death itself I do not fear; for it is quick. I have escaped it often

enough in the past to know that. It is the awful waiting for the
blow, and the uncertainty of when it will fall . . . . (pp. 187–88)

Luftwaffe attrition is in direct proportion to RAF success, making the respective memoirs inverses of each other. As C. F. Rawnsley
gains self-confidence with the improved performance of his AI equipment, the pace of *Night Fighter* quickens; Peter Stahl's *The Diving
Eagle,* on the other hand, suffers the counterpoint of growing losses
that result from the better skill of British night fighters and antiaircraft gunners. Stahl is one of the luckier pilots, having logged sixty
missions against England, most of them in easier times; as he writes in
mid 1941, the loss rate is taking new crews after just three or four
night operations. German night fighters suffer the same rate of casualties. Wilhelm Johnen notes in *Duel Under the Stars* that "Night
after night the youngsters did not return while the veterans continued
to pile up their victories" (p. 66). Such attrition is not immediately
catastrophic, but the pool of skilled pilots cannot last forever when
recruits meant to replenish it are being steadily drained away.

RAF Fighter Command twice faces severe hardship: during the
Battle of France and at the height of the Battle of Britain. The first
challenge is beaten off politically. Dowding takes his case directly to
the top and eventually persuades Churchill that if any more squadrons are sent to France, where they face sure annihilation, Britain will
be left defenseless after its ally's certain fall. With a bare minimum of
forces kept intact for the summer's battle, Fighter Command begins a
war not only with the Luftwaffe but with its own numbers. Can
enough new Spitfires and Hurricanes be supplied to bring squadron
strength back above fifty from its June low of twenty-six? Lord
Beaverbook's system of shadow factories (private industries, largely
auto makers, licensed to produce the Supermarine and Hawker
fighters), combined with a fantastically efficient repair scheme,
guarantees that there will be no immediate shortage of aircraft, so the
main contest becomes the race for pilots. Training is accelerated, and
replacements arrive with less than ten hours of flying time on Spitfires
or Hurricanes, while experienced pilots must be borrowed from the
Fleet Air Arm and Coastal Command. The crunch comes in the two
weeks surrounding September 1, as 200 more planes are lost than
received and 231 of the 1,000 pilots available are killed, wounded, or
missing in action. With six of the seven sector airfields badly damaged
and the northerly Groups unable to rotate because they are depleted
of well-rested squadrons, Fighter Command finds its back to the wall.

Dowding and Park now make certain tactical moves to minimize losses, but their principal means of salvation comes from Hitler and Göring, who change the focus of their attack from the RAF to London. With the capital accepting the losses, squadron and pilot strength is rebuilt and the German offensive is fought off.

Individual losses are borne best in the matter-of-fact, kill-or-be-killed mood that the fighter style demands for its emotional survival. Of all the memoirists only Pierre Closterman with his heightened visual responsiveness devotes as much detail to the crashes of friends as to those of enemies. In one incident a colleague in a Hurricane is killed instantly, but his plane flies on in a steep climb:

> At the top of the trajectory one wing wilted, the aircraft hung as on a thread suspended in space motionless, then went into a spin.
>
> As in a nightmare I saw Warrant Officer Pearce's Hurricane literally mown down by a burst of 37 mm. The tail came off, the machine crashed into a wood, scything down the trees, scattering jets of burning petrol.
>
> The other two Hurricanes attacked simultaneously. Struck by a direct hit, Sergeant Clive's machine exploded and was soon nothing but an inchoate mass of flame, dragging a long trail of black smoke. (p. 69)

Closterman's eye can separate the action and sort out the details, since no two losses are even remotely similar except in their suddenness. Not that less hurried losses are easier to bear, for the process only retards Closterman's narrative into a hideously slow motion. A disabled Spitfire drifts past in a shallow dive, its propeller stationary and its radiator streaming glycol. The squadron letters spell out a breathless message to Closterman—it is a close friend—and he frantically calls to him to bail out. But there is no response from the crumpled shape within, and Closterman must close his eyes as the plane's dive steepens "as if it was trying to do an outside loop." A moment later there is "Nothing left but a blazing mass by a roadside" (p. 117). Later in the war, when he is flying Tempests, difficult aircraft to land when they are disabled, Closterman sees a friend consumed in a fiery crash. Soon he himself survives a similar wreck; but when a third plane crashes with its engine afire he simply assents to another flier's cynical refusal to rush to the site—"Christ, what's the hurry? There can't be much left" (p. 206).

Losses, whether accepted tacitly or described in just detail, are an inevitable part of the fighter style. Simply flying such machines dictates the risk, and some of the most spectacular crashes happen far away from combat. Douglas Bader survives his, but he loses both his legs and endangers his service career (which he regains only later when the RAF is strapped for experienced pilots). The combination of low-level aerobatics and the beat-up of one's airfield, all meant to impress one's squadron friends, nearly takes his life. It does prove fatal to the war's first hero, Flying Officer Cobber Cain, who concludes his brave service in the Battle of France by taking up his Hurricane for a final display, even as a Magister communications plane waits to fly him back to England. As Noel Monks records in *Squadrons Up!*, the charismatic Cain's last words are, "Cheerio, chaps. Be good." With the waiting Magister ticking over, he leaps into his Hurricane for one last circuit, consisting of an inverted pass at an altitude of twenty feet and at three hundred sixty miles per hour followed by a climb to fifteen hundred feet and two diving rolls:

> Two rolls are completed. The group of RAF officers suddenly stops laughing and chattering. One says anxiously, "What the hell?" as the Hurricane goes into a third roll, which his experienced eye can see will bring it mighty close to earth. Then three or four of them yell, "Cobber, Cobber," and start running. There's a crash. The Hurricane doesn't quite complete the third roll. The port wing touches the ground. . . .
>
> While the young officers are lifting their dead comrade from the wreckage, a mechanic climbs into the cockpit of the Magister. He switches off the engine. (p. 5)

Monks, as the first war correspondent to become close friends with the new style of pilots, appreciates how the same recklessness that would compromise a bomber crew becomes, for the fighter pilot, "a virtue. Fighting alone in his flying bullet, he can afford to be reckless. It gets him out of tight corners at times" (p. 29). For Bader, joining a new squadron, and for Cain, bidding farewell to the station where he has become a hero, the challenge is to stretch the necessary risk of their profession to its extreme: one last gravity-defying roll closer to the ground than any man has tried before. That the gambit fails leaves the impossibility of perfection intact. Though Monks will continue for two hundred sixty pages to recount the episodes of Cain's grand career, the opening pages of the book are reserved for the drama of this pilot's death, the style of which becomes the key element in his life, which the purity of the fighter style insures he will not survive.

5
Bomber Command

I N both style and substance the bomber war is entirely different
from fighter combat. Few contrasts are greater than that of a
nimble Spitfire darting through the clouds and a heavy Lancaster
lumbering off toward Germany. Distinctions in size, performance,
and mission, such as the added responsibility of a seven-man crew
and the moral questions raised by destroying not just military targets
but civilian population centers, have a dramatic effect on the style of
flying. At the highest echelon there is a struggle—not Dowding's and
Park's heroic defense of Great Britain but Air Chief Marshal Sir
Arthur Harris's unglorious mission to convince the government that
the strategic destruction of the enemy's ability to wage war, including
the devastation of its economic base, was the only way to ensure
victory. In the middle range of command occasions arise for distinguished action, such as the brave role of the Pathfinder force and the
gallantry of the dam buster squadron. But for the most part the
bomber offensive reveals a far more stolid and even plodding style of
combat than was seen in fighter warfare, one in which a flier with the
specialized job of navigator, bomb aimer, flight engineer, gunner, or
pilot of a large and complex machine patiently counts his missions as
Germany burns below.

The ambiguous role of bomber warfare, which leaves little room
for the iconography of heroism so common to the fighter style,
prompts recriminations from both sides. Luftwaffe memoirists complain that their own bombing of England did not amount to a fraction
of the terror unleashed on Germany three and four years later. Bomb
tonnage supports this claim, as does an analysis of the two air forces.
The Luftwaffe was equipped with only medium-range, medium-
weight bombers designed for tactical support of an advancing army.
The bomber force owed its form to such chance factors as the un-

timely death in 1936 of General Walther Wever, who had developed plans for a long-range, four-engine bomber, and the ascendancy of General Ernst Udet, whose fascination with American dive-bombers led in 1933 to the mandate that all Luftwaffe bombers have diving capability, which severely limited their size, power, range, capacity, and speed. In 1940 the Luftwaffe's proud image was that of the Stuka dive-bomber, an ikon quickly smashed by RAF fighter strength, and for the rest of the war German bombing power continued to diminish. The RAF bomber forces, however, continued to grow in size and number, from Whitleys and Hamptons through Halifaxes and Stirlings to the mighty Lancaster, hailed as the finest heavy bomber ever built. Designed for long-range strategic bombing, Harris's force carried more destruction to Germany than any nation has suffered in modern warfare, all accomplished in a spirit of clockwork and target attrition that seemed like the workings of a gigantic machine. It is no wonder that the German memoirists picture themselves as fighting something larger than human invention, though they launch ample indictments against the human spirit that turned it loose.

Not that the RAF story lacks recriminations against the Germans. In *Duel of Eagles,* which begins with its author bringing down the war's first German bomber on English soil, Peter Townsend adds the explanation that "Strategic bombing or, more realistically, total air warfare, is a German invention, though in their turn the English later directed it against Germany" (p. 12). Townsend's language slips into swollen rhetoric when, after citing the 1915 bombing of London, he introduces the 1940 Blitz by warning that "For the second time in twenty-five years the Germans were out to subdue the British with their own Teutonic invention, murder from the sky" (p. 397). Townsend's perspective is that of a fighter pilot. Bomber Command memoirs remain largely free of such inflammatory prose; instead, their tone is one of regretful apocalypse. Russell Braddon's *Cheshire V. C.,* a biography of the famous bomber pilot Leonard Cheshire, begins with Cheshire's last mission in the war—to observe the nuclear bombing of Nagasaki (an experience which Braddon maintains changed Cheshire's life), and Sir Arthur Harris concludes his own memoir, *Bomber Offensive,* with a prophecy of atomic ICBM warfare. "My part in the next war," he judges grimly in 1947, "will be to be destroyed in it; I cannot doubt that if there is a war within the next quarter century it will certainly destroy a very great part of the civilized world and disrupt it entirely" (p. 280).

A contributing factor to the bomber's ambiguity as an ikon for the war is the history of its use against civilian targets. For the first nine months of the war Hitler had forbidden the Luftwaffe from bombing targets in England, a product of his own rhetoric that the English people were not his natural enemy and that he would rather coax them into an armistice than alienate them by attacks. Even in the first months of fighting in the summer of 1940 the German bomber groups kept away from civilian targets. But on August 24 twelve crews strayed from their objective, the aircraft factories at Rochester and Kingston and the oil refineries at Thameshaven, all at least twenty miles from London, and instead bombed neighborhoods within the capital itself. Hitler was furious—he ordered that the offending airmen be transferred to the infantry—but not as furious as Churchill, who in what several American correspondents described as "a fit of pique" announced that Berlin was to be bombed the next night. Bomber Command struck the German capital on August 25 and again on August 28 and 30. Reporting from Berlin, William L. Shirer noted the stunned disillusionment of people who had trusted Göring's boast that "If an enemy bomber reaches the Ruhr, my name is not Hermann Göring: you can call me Meier!" The Reichsmarshal was now being called "Meier" all over Germany, and Hitler was conscious that his own reputation was at stake. Within a week the Führer signed the order declaring civilian London a target—the blitz was on, and it would not stop until the end of World War II itself with the bombing of Hiroshima and Nagasaki. In Churchill's memoirs there are no regrets; instead, he likens London to a great prehistoric monster capable of suffering all sorts of terrible injuries and still living on. There is some speculation among British historians that his reprisal attacks on Berlin were meant to encourage a Luftwaffe blitz and thereby divert the German attack from the RAF airfields, which were near collapse, and to involve the British people more directly in the war, for which their spirit had flagged.

This strategy was first expounded in the work of Italian general Giulio Douhet, whose theories informed the thinking of British and German bombing planners alike. As Len Deighton judges in *Fighter,* "It was the pressure that civilians under air bombardment would put upon their own government that formed the basis of Douhet's theories" (p. 54). The London and Berlin reprisals are just such factors, with the added twist of Churchill using them to inflame British opinion just as Hitler intended the opposite. Lord Trenchard in Britain and General Billy Mitchell in the United States spent the decades between the two world wars arguing the case for strategic bombing, a policy of defeating not the enemy's army but its nation. Trenchard's words were frank: "It is in the destruction of enemy industries and, above all, on the lowering of morale of enemy nationals caused by bombing, that ultimate victory rests." Politicians, for once, spoke even more frankly, Clement Attlee admitting that since the bomber would always get through, "the only defense is an offense, which means that you have to kill more women and children more quickly than the enemy if you want to save yourselves." A commander such as Harris acted and spoke apocalyptically, scraping together relatively ineffective training units to swell the ranks for a "Thousand Bomber" raid on Cologne and soon after imploring Churchill, with words Allen Andrews, in *The Air Marshals,* says sound like a papal encyclical, that "Victory, speedy and complete, awaits the side which first employs air power as it should be employed" (p. 213). Harris felt that the bomber would be the definitive weapon of the Second World War, as the submarine had been of the First. He considered a good offense to be the best defense and in his memoir discredited the idea of defense as "a gesture not of war but of inferiority" (Harris, p. 278).

Harris makes an overwhelming case for the heavy bomber as a strategic tool, the only weapon capable of preventing Germany from crossing the Channel. Fighters could conduct only the defensive side of the war, whereas Bomber Command offered the sole means then available of carrying the war to the enemy; therefore Inskip's policy of reliance on fighters had to be readjusted in favor of rebuilding the bomber force in a plane-for-plane production race. Writing less than two years after the war's end, Harris can already marshal a great deal of history in support of his position. He offers the valid assessment that without his bombers' attacks on the launch sites of the V-1 and V-2 rockets London would have been devastated by these weapons, and that had the Germans managed to prolong the war they might have brought atomic warfare into the European theater.

The bomber offensive against Germany began in earnest on February 14, 1942, with innovations in equipment and strategy: a radar navigation aid called Gee, which could guide bombers accurately up to four hundred miles from base, and a commitment to destroy—not just harass—the industrial cities of Essen, Duisberg, Dusseldorf, and Cologne. When Harris assumed command on February 22, the air war over Germany took a new, destructive turn, one that sparked a controversy that continues to this day. Although the targets were industrial centers, the true purpose of these raids loomed large, as Harris candidly explains: "The general ideas at this time on what civil servants always call 'a high level,' was that the main and almost only purpose of bombing was to attack the morale of the industrial workers. This was to be achieved by destroying, mainly by incendiary bombs, the whole of the four largest cities in the Ruhr, and thereafter fourteen industrial cities elsewhere in Germany" (p. 76). Harris criticized this policy as the counsel of despair prompted by the failure of earlier night precision bombings, and he argued that to be effective his bomber force must become large in number and concentrated in effect and above all not be frittered away on diverse targets. Civilian areas should not be exempt, but they should be destroyed all the more thoroughly with heavy concentrations of bombs "starting so many fires at the same time that no firefighting services, however efficiently and quickly they were reinforced by the fire brigades of other towns, could get them under control" (p. 83). Here is the source for that most devastating part of the bomber war's image—the fire storm, an event of pyrotechnic engineering that killed hundreds of thousands in Hamburg and Dresden. The key to creating a fire storm was to launch concentrated area attacks, and though unpopular with the American allies, they proved to be effective (Harris notes smugly that American B-29s adopted the same practice against Japan). These great destructive raids had to wait until 1944, however, for most of Bomber Command's growth in Harris's first year on the job was drawn off to fill other needs around the world. Even in the final year of the war there were tactical drains, such as specific attacks on the ball bearing industry (which Harris argued was so widely dispersed as to be invulnerable), but by 1944 the giant machine of Bomber Command was ready to engulf Germany in explosion and flame.

The candor of a man like Harris can be used against him, as Adolf Galland does in *The First and the Last* when he offers his own indictment of the bomber offensive:

> Hardly a day and rarely a night passed without heavy raids, mostly by more than 1000 four-engined bombers. One German town after another sank into ruins. In his memoirs "Bomber" Harris says: "It must be expressively mentioned that, except for Essen, we never chose any particular factory as a target. The destruction of industrial plants was always regarded as a special task. Our aim was always the center of town." [So reads Mervyn Savill's retranslation of Galland's rendering into German. The original quote, from p. 147 of *Bomber Offensive*, reads in context: "But it must be emphasized that in no instance, except in

Essen, were we aiming specifically at any one factory in the Battle of the Ruhr; the destruction of factories, which was nevertheless on an enormous scale, could be regarded as a bonus. The aiming points were usually right in the center of town; the average German city had spread outwards from an old center, which was naturally more densely built-up than the newer and well-planned suburbs; it was this densely built-up center which was most susceptible to area attack with incendiary bombs. The objective of the campaign was to reduce production in the industries of the Ruhr at least as much by indirect effect as damage to services, housing, and amenities, as by any direct damage to the factories or railways themselves."] Thus in most German towns it was always the center with its culture, hundreds or even thousands of years old, that was destroyed, and the modern industrial districts, which resemble each other all over the world, although they received some damage, remained more or less intact. (p. 287)

Hence the ambiguity of Britain's bomber offensive, which invites remarkably divergent opinions from an RAF Air Chief Marshal and a Luftwaffe General of Fighters who disagree on everything from the meaning of urban geography to the importance of culture and history.

Such doings may seem the stuff of politics and high strategy, but concerns about ethics and effectiveness work their way down through the ranks to color the experiences of pilots and crews. A great portion of Peter Townsend's night fighter memoir *Duel in the Dark* is devoted to the blitz on London. To examine the consequences of Churchill's Berlin reprisal and Hitler's order to turn his bombers against London, Townsend shifts his narrative focus from the fighter stations (against which Luftwaffe attacks had been most frequent in August) to Woolwich, a neighborhood in the East End, where the Callow family endures the worst of the bombing. As the daytime attacks of September 7 continue into the night, Townsend turns his attention to the skies above the burning London streets:

The fading daylight brought no reprieve to the firemen. Night bombers were streaming up the estuary towards London. Hauptmann Hajo Hermann, piloting a Junkers 88 bomber, remarked: "A very clear night. Everything was lit up by fires, like a huge torch in the night." Until that night Luftwaffe aircrews had obeyed strict orders against indiscriminate bombing. Now they simply tipped their bombs into the sea of flame and smoke below. (p. 72)

With the new bombing practices in action, metaphors soon arise to describe them, seas of flame into which more destruction is tipped as from a witch's cauldron. But Townsend is careful to keep analysis at hand as well; thus he points out how the use of parachuted land mines, which are utterly undirectable once released, could turn "young men, decent and brave and good in themselves, into callous murderers of innocent people," an act which marks "the first step in the willful, wholesale massacre of civilians" (p. 88). When a captured crewman from the Coventry raid reveals that one entire unit had been ordered to drop its bombs not on factories but on workers' housing, Townsend's record for indictment is complete, with the city's ruined Cathedral serving as an ikon of the bombers' ruthless devastation.

Townsend is a fighter pilot, but one of the most highly decorated bomber pilots of the war, Guy Gibson, takes time in *Enemy Coast Ahead* to share his fighter squadron colleagues' dismay at what bombing can do. His specific case is a surprising one, but therefore all the more effective for its inclusion of the air war's central mythology. He journeys down to the corner of Kent famous for its bucolic fighter bases, from which men like Bader and Johnson could climb to twenty-five thousand feet and fight a cleaner and more noble war. Gibson has kind words for the lush hop country with its charming old pubs and friendly, hardworking people. It is a lovely region all year round:

> But in Kent the beginning of May is a sight to be seen. No one could have given this fair country a better name than the "Garden of England." As we flew over the orchards on our way to the 'drome we saw the apple-blossom was out. White and fragrant, it gave the impression of newly formed snow. One by one the orchards came and went in continuous panorama, some large, some small, but all owned by the men of Kent. Now and then an oast-house would flash by. This is where the hops are dried, and they say you can feel tight on the smell alone if you stay in long enough. And all over the country was the Mark of the Beast — thousands of bomb craters that had left their holes in the white chalk, dropped in neat sticks miles from anywhere. This, we found out later, was known as the jettison area where many a windy Hun, pursued by fighters, would pull the plug, then leg it for home across the Channel. (p. 139)

Thus even the most pastoral of RAF images, their lovely Kentish countryside from which the fliers quest as noble knights, is devastated by "the Beast," which Bomber Command, in its own beastliness, will have to annihilate.

If there is a bomber spirit to complement the fighter style, it derives from several elements: the high risk of missions flown over great distances through enemy night fighters and flak, the high odds against surviving an operational tour, and the moral pressure of doing such destructive work. But whatever the cause, the results show themselves in a special consciousness of the crew and one's role within it. Fighter pilots faced the enemy both psychologically and physically as individuals; while such conditions enhanced the pilot's effectiveness, it is certain that the bomber's work would become a much heavier moral burden were responsibility for it placed on just one man. A crew of seven was itself a small society responding as a group to an enemy society's attack on their own. And just as none of the members of a firing squad know who has fired the fatal bullet, no single crewman of a Lancaster need feel individually responsible for the destruction being rained down below. The bombardier simply aimed bombs carried to the spot by six fellow crewmen; the pilot was no longer singly responsible, for half the plane's controls were operated by the flight engineer; both these men were dependent on the guidance of their navigator and wireless operator; and as essential as any was the role of the air gunners, who kept their Lancaster itself from becoming a victim. This interdependency and mutual support answers Pierre Closterman's complaint about the fighter pilot's anxious isolation, for here in the bomber each man had the comforting feeling of being surrounded by other men, a feeling that was denied to the solitary airman in his Hurricane or Spitfire.

The typical fighter narrative begins with its protagonist being shot down; most bomber memoirs start with the author forming his crew, for on this day the wartime experience assumes its form. This is how Jack Currie inaugurates *Lancaster Target,* as scores of other airmen mill about in the drill hangar:

> I stood among the other sergeant-pilots and, trying not to stare at anyone in particular, looked round the assembled groups of aircrew. There were bomb-aimers, navigators, wireless-operators and gunners, and I needed one of each to form my crew. I didn't know any of them; up to now my Air Force world had been peopled by pilots. This was a crowd of strangers. I had a sudden recollection of standing in a suburban dance-hall, wondering which girl I should approach. I remembered that it wasn't always

the prettiest or smartest girl who made the best companion for the evening. Anyway, this wasn't the same as choosing a dancing partner; it was more like picking out a sweetheart or a wife, for better or for worse. I needed four of these men to fly with, live with, go to war with. If, as I planned, we went on from Wellingtons to heavy bombers, I would have to find another gunner and an engineer later in our training, but the five of us who came together now would be the nucleus of the crew. (p. 7)

The crew forms up along the lines of another simile, eye contact between two of the men leading to the second's suggestion of a third man he knows — "Have you got a bomb-aimer? I know a good one" — all of whom are joined by a fourth, inviting them for a cup of tea. And so just as any small social group might form, the bomber crew takes shape. What begins casually, however, cements itself into strong group loyalty, another drawing upon of everyday human behavior that contributes to the strength of these crews. In *Only Owls and Bloody Fools Fly at Night* Group Captain Tom Sawyer explains the benefits of this system:

> It was at this stage that the really tremendous crew spirit was created. Once a crew had decided to fly together — and the trainee intakes were left to themselves to pick their own crews from amongst themselves — then that was it. For ever after they only wanted to fly with each other, and when circumstances forced them to fly with other crews, generally through sickness of one of them, then they really did not like it. And therefore when a crew got through a whole bomber tour together — which soon became a rare occurrence — it was the same crew which had started together early on in their OTU [Operational Training Unit] days. (p. 19)

Crewing up provides the first structure for bomber narratives, one that remains durable right to the end. The crew of Miles Tripp's *The Eighth Passenger* is not only one of the lucky ones to survive a thirty-operation tour, but it remains intact through the Catch-22s near the war's end, which for a time continually raise the number of missions needed to complete a tour. "Listen to this," the pilot tells the crew, "An order came through today that any crew which hadn't completed twenty-five ops by this morning will have to fly an extra five before being tour-expired. That means us. We did our twenty-fifth a few hours too late" (p. 74). One day and one mission later, the total is raised from thirty to forty, until near the end of the narrative's wartime phase the author admits, "I had ceased counting the numbers of operations left in our extended tour. So far as I could see, we should go on flying until we were killed and there wasn't any point in teasing oneself with the prospect of ultimate safety" (p. 89). Yet when, unbelievably, their fortieth and final operation concludes, the most amazing thing happens. "From the mêlée of Lancasters our squadron began formating"—on their own plane's tail. "It was the first time we had ever flown back in formation," Tripp remarks, and adds with wonder that when approaching the airfield the accompanying aircraft peel off to give them the honor of landing first, alone. For the last time the pilot and flight engineer read through the landing drill, and before the plane empties the crew members fix the scene in memory. Even here the narrative is only half-complete. The structure of crewing up lies dormant through two postwar decades, until an inquiry by Mike Garbett, doing research for the first of his *Lancaster at War* books, spurs Miles Tripp to find his old crew members and to collate their own stories and reactions with his. These form the book's second section, in which the nature of the bomber crew family is detailed. Yet history demands still more narratives, and as the crew is brought together one more time for a documentary about the air war being filmed by West German television, Miles Tripp's wife dies suddenly.

Forming crews creates a complex structure, for relationships among the seven fliers are factored to the seventh power, making forty-nine personal stories for every one of Fighter Command's. With the mix of nationalities provided by the Empire Training Plan and with transfers from the various Dominion air forces, the dramatic possibilities are multipled as the range of character types is broadened. Flight Lieutenant Walter Thompson is a Canadian pilot who tells of his RAF service in *Lancaster to Berlin*. His attempt to form a crew of unmarried men runs afoul when three of his choices turn out to have fibbed to him; instead of himself selecting all the crew members, his wireless operator chooses him. This man, Andy Wilkes, recommends a bomb aimer who looks none too presentable:

> I wasn't too certain of him and asked if I could see his log book. I leafed through it, not seeing any proficiency assessments and asked him his name. "Hanratty is my name," he said, belligerently avoiding the use of the word "sir." I said, "Fine Hanratty, would you join my crew?" "Just a moment," he said in a strong Scottish accent, "Let me see your log book." He rolled

the "r" in "your" and pronounced book "bewk." Taken a little aback I handed the book to him and watched him thumb through its pages with yellow fingers. The examination apparently satisfied his pride, if not his curiosity. He handed it back and said, "All right, I'll come with you but only because you're not an Englishman," again rolling the "r." He looked and acted like "Grumpy" in "Snow White and the Seven Dwarfs." I turned to Wilkes and asked softly, "What's he got against the English?" Wilkes said, "Oh, he's just worried that he might have to salute an English pilot and call him sir. He swears he won't do it—and he's afraid he'll be put on charge for refusing to do it. He thinks it will be different with a Canadian." (pp. 41–42)

In action a bomber crew offers a broad spectrum of responses to its mission. Early in *Enemy Coast Ahead* (a title that evokes the thrill and trepidation of the crew at the bomb aimer's fateful announcement) Guy Gibson spends one flight remarking on the different personalities at work: his wireless operator flashing an Aldis light message that they all should get drunk the next night, the rear gunner helping plot drift, the navigator happy once he can settle down to his quiet plotting in seclusion, emerging from behind the blackout curtains to deliver a comical rendition of his own service to the pilot— "Our ground speed is 203½ miles per hour; we will be there in exactly one hour and ten minutes, thirty seconds. We ought to cross the coast dead on track, so everything's fine. Incidentally, you're one degree off your course" (p. 21). Gibson is amazed to discover that the plane is flying seven different missions, thanks to the diverse interests and perceptions of his crew. An hour out of England with still another hour remaining before they cross the European coast, Gibson considers the dozen and a half other Lancasters that accompany them and is struck by the thought that "here are 133 boys who have got an hour to live before going through hell. Some of them won't get back. It won't be me—you never think that you are not coming back. We won't all get back, but who is it will be unlucky out of these 133 men? What are they thinking about?" (p. 22). With the hindsight of memory Gibson continues with a ghastly paragraph, wondering what the rear gunner in Melvyn Young's plane might be thinking, because he will not be coming back. Neither will another rear gunner who bails out and spends the balance of the war in a prison camp with his bomb aimer, the only two of this crew to survive. Gibson asks what he is doing here himself, who so lately was sailing off a holiday beach when summoned by telegram back to his bomber station. The date then had been August 31, 1939. Now it was May 16, 1943, and he was flying a possible suicide mission against the massive Moehne and Eder dams. Much history had already elapsed, but in terms of action and destruction even more was to follow. Written and published during the war, *Enemy Coast Ahead* plots the bomber war faithfully — and tragically, for Gibson himself would not survive it.

Dam busting and the precision target marking of the Pathfinder Force proved to be the two specific tasks that both answered the moral questions about bombing and allowed individual skill and personal exploits to show themselves so prominently. The famous bomber pilots — Guy Gibson, Leonard Cheshire, Don Bennett — distinguished themselves in these roles, and although the most representative stories remain those in such memoirs as Don Charlwood's *No Moon Tonight* (told from the navigator's point of view) and Jack Currie's *Lancaster Target* (subtitled "the story of a crew who flew from Wickenby"), certain facets of the dam buster and Pathfinder experiences shed light on the most troublesome and also most interesting features of the bomber war. Significantly, Air Chief Marshal Harris opposed the formation of both — of the dam busters because he didn't want scientists playing with the lives of his already hard-suffering bomber boys, and of the Pathfinders because he opposed the idea of an elite force.

Paul Brickhill's *The Dam Busters* is the central text for the first, and its front matter raises the issues this style of attack addresses: not just the demonstration of how small yet highly trained numbers can overcome a much larger force, as the author explains in his "Briefing," but Marshal of the RAF Arthur Tedder's claim that the dam busters' success refutes any charge that bombing must be indiscriminate and must be devoted to destruction for destruction's sake. Early on Brickhill cites the classic example of such bombing — the German bombardment of villages in the Spanish Civil War — and posits his own ideal to replace it: "A few such bombs accurately aimed might shatter the roots of a nation's war effort. That could mean the end of the dreadful 'Guernica' carpet bombing, which wiped out cities and civilians at the same time" (p. 10). By now Guernica had become more than a devastated Spanish market town; it was a horrific painting by Pablo Picasso and a code word for bombing's mass slaughter of the innocent. To efface that image another ikon must be painted in its place, and this is what Brickhill, in *The Dam Busters,* and Gibson, in the latter pages of *Enemy Coast Ahead,* undertake to do.

Much of the dam-busting effort owes its success to the high

science of Barnes Wallis, designer of the Wellesley and Wellington bombers and a man fascinated with the prospects of a massive "earthquake bomb" capable of unsettling the largest concrete structures in the world. To put these bombs down where they were needed, at base level between the towers of the mighty Moehne dam from a height of sixty feet above the water, two essentially primitive tools were fashioned. To maintain such a low-tolerance altitude at night, two searchlights were affixed to the Lancasters and aimed so that their beams intersected at sixty feet. In order to sight on the dam's twin towers, a triangle of plywood was cut with a peephole looking out at two nails; when the towers lined up with the nails, the bomber had reached the release point. Each of these improvisations worked as well as the ten-ton bomb Barnes Wallis had developed to do the damage.

The dam-busting squadron, formed in secret by Gibson, is a microcosmic and intensely highbred version of bomber operations. Nearly every man recruited wore high decorations, yet their average age was twenty-two, a testament to the pressures of warfare and the opportunities for valor, which had elevated Gibson to Wing Commander and Cheshire (the next special unit commander) to Group Captain before the age of twenty-five. From the depths of midwar exhaustion the sight of these men renews Gibson's enthusiasm, just as the mission itself is meant to revitalize the bomber offensive:

> There were twenty-one crews, comprising 147 men: pilots, navigators, wireless-operators, bomb-aimers, flight engineers. Nearly all of them twenty-three years old or under, and nearly all of them veterans. I saw them in the same old crew room, which brought back many memories of 1939–40 days. Now it was packed full of young, carefree-looking boys, mostly blue-eyed, keen and eager to hear the gen. I felt quite old among them. (p. 230)

All aspects of the raid are top secret, from the engineers and technicians who build the bomb in sections, no one man knowing all facets of the work, to the crews who train on various abstract exercises, none of which implies the nature of the final target. Gibson alone knows the full story, probably the only time in the war one bomber pilot has held so much individual responsibility and control. The target is equally awesome: the Moehne and Eder dams, with walls 140 feet thick and 150 feet high holding back a 12-mile-long lake containing 140 million tons of water. The stakes of such a raid are equally high. The Allies' Casablanca Conference had recently decreed that the bomber war against Germany must destroy not just Germany's military forces but everything needed to build, support, and replace those forces, including the nation's industrial capacity, economic structure, and civilian morale. The Moehne and Eder dams were ideal targets; destroying them not only would be an apocalyptic spectacle sure to shock the populace but would greatly reduce industrial production in the Ruhr, for it took eight tons of water to produce just one ton of steel.

Planning and training for this raid epitomize the intense effort of all the schools and Operational Training Units, and its execution brings together every element of a bomber attack, except now both exceptionally concise in focus yet magnified in results: the trepidation, the fateful attrition, the struggle through night fighters and ground defenses, and the eerie concentration of the bomb run, here centered on one of the war's most precise aiming points. The talents of each crew member are tested to the limit. Gibson's narrative is one of the most exciting accounts of the air war, couched as it is within his confessed feeling of his aircraft being "so small" and the dam "so large; it was thick and solid, and now it was angry. My aircraft was very small" (p. 274). Even the squadron's losses are more awesome:

> "M Mother" was on fire; an unlucky shot had got him in one of the inboard petrol tanks and a long jet of flame was beginning to stream out. I saw him drop his mine, but his bomb-aimer must have been wounded, because it fell straight on to the power-house on the other side of the dam. But Hoppy staggered on, trying to gain altitude so that his crew could bale out. When he had got up to about 500 feet there was a livid flash in the sky and one wing fell off; his aircraft disintegrated and fell to the ground in cascading, flaming fragments. There it began to burn quite gently and rather sinisterly in a field some three miles beyond the dam. (p. 275)

The close observation of these friends' deaths, packed with emotional description as it is, is complemented and redeemed in the dam's destruction. To describe the wall breaking, Gibson resorts to a simile as surprising as he finds the event itself to be: "there was a great breach 100 yards across, and the water, looking like stirred porridge in the moonlight, was gushing out and rolling into the Ruhr Valley." The valley fills with fog rising from this foamy torrent of water, ahead of which Gibson sees cars vainly trying to outrun it:

> I saw their headlights burning and I saw water overtake them, wave by wave, and then the color of the headlights underneath the water changing from light blue to green, from green to dark purple, until there was no longer anything except the water bouncing down in great waves. The floods raced on, carrying with them as they went — viaducts, railways, bridges and everything that stood in their path. Three miles beyond the dam the remains of Hoppy's aircraft were still burning gently, a dull red glow on the ground. Hoppy had been avenged. (p. 277)

Among the most literary of Bomber Command narratives, Gibson's description evokes a world like the one seen by Mark Twain's narrator in *The Mysterious Stranger,* where the things of mankind are destroyed as if they were toys by a power from above. Although an area bombing raid causes more destruction, it lacks such centers of focus, both in the air and on the ground, to make such description possible.

The dam busting created legends and generated texts, from the drama of Gibson's serious wartime memoir to the comedy of a bogus letter to the *Times* of London protesting the loss of two nesting ringnecked whooper swans — "assuming that this operation was necessary, could it not have been deferred until the cygnets (if any) were full grown?" — to pilot Mick Martin's answer to a request for a mission souvenir: "Sir, I am very interested in your museum and am sending you, enclosed, the Moehne Dam." Martin's letter bore a curious postscript: "Opened by censors and contents confiscated by the Metropolitan Water Board" (Brickhill, *The Dam Busters,* pp. 76–77).

The dam buster squadron remained active to the end of the war. Under the command of Leonard Cheshire, who succeeded Guy Gibson, it conducted an elaborate radar feint, which simulated a phantom invasion fleet on D-Day; it smashed heavily fortified submarine and E-boat pens, canals, and the threatening V-series rocket sites, including those of the little-known V-3, intended to shell London with huge artillery projectiles from the Continent. A key target was the V-1 and V-2 research station at Peenemünde, where another top-secret raid retarded the development of these weapons for a crucial six to nine months but in the process, because of some misaiming, killed six hundred slave laborers and a group of deported Luxembourgers who had been secreting out intelligence on the weapons to British agents. This was not the only mistake; the crews had been told they were attacking a new installation for radar-controlled night fighters (a nemesis sure to boost their commitment) and that if the attack were unsuccessful they would have to remount it on succeeding nights. Word was leaked of this latter threat, and so the Germans used camouflage to simulate a complete knockout and thus saved much of the facility. A diversion to Berlin, however, proved successful and drew off the night fighters (as Wilhem Johnen laments in *Duel Under the Stars*), and so the dam busters persevered with their fame intact.

Leonard Cheshire's contribution to the special squadron was an exceptionally accurate technique of low-level target marking. No matter how well the larger force hit the markers, if those flares were not where they should be, the entire raid's effect would, by its very precision, miscarry. Cheshire argued his case directly to Air Chief Marshal Harris with what biographer Russell Braddon characterizes as the skill "one would expect from the son of one of Britain's finest jurists and legal writers, and one who had himself, though reluctantly, studied Law" at Oxford:

> He pointed out that high-level marking in heavy bombers meant starting one's run-in on the target from perhaps as far away as twenty miles whence any pin-point landmark would well be invisible and must be oblique. Even granted the best of visibility, however, the most skilled high-level bomb-aimers were unlikely to drop their markers with the accuracy required. The oncoming stream of bombers might then drop their explosives three or four hundred yards from the markers . . . and the target would remain unscathed.
>
> Accuracy of marking, therefore, obviously depended upon a low attack, where visibility would be reasonable at least, and where such factors as drift were negligible. But low attacks inevitably involved flying through very heavy hostile fire in the claws of equally hostile searchlights; and to this the ponderous Lancasters would be tragically vulnerable. Even at 5,000 feet which Cheshire, with his hatred of heights, considered not nearly low enough, a heavy bomber was still not accurate enough and was also extremely vulnerable to light flak. They must fly in even lower and mark even more accurately. Four *hundred* feet was more like it and frequently, in the raids that followed, Cheshire marked at fifty feet from the ground.
>
> Cheshire later summed it up thus: the dropping of markers

(those colored pin-points on the ground which became the actual bombers' only target in a holocaust of flak, searchlights and darkness) is the function of a low-flying aircraft. But Lancasters are designed to function at a great height. Therefore, Lancasters should *not* be used to mark the target: a fast, light, manoeuvrable plane should take their place. That plane, added Cheshire, was a Mosquito. (Bradden, pp. 106–7)

Cheshire's struggle for Mosquito resources fits the individualism of his special unit. First he proves the benefits of low-level dives, albeit in the ridiculously unsuitable heavy Lancaster; then he accepts a gamble from Harris that if the Mosquitoes guide a raid successfully to one of his most elusive targets, Munich, Cheshire can have the planes he wants. The marking is perfect, the raid a success, and Harris responds not just with the four Mosquitoes Cheshire requested but with an entire squadron of these coveted planes, plus two squadrons of Lancasters from the Pathfinders. From now on the dam busters would operate as pathfinders to the Pathfinders, a virtual Group by itself.

At this point the dam busters' and Pathfinders' interests cross, and while jealousy between them remains, the identical spirit motivates their remarkable successes. Before the war was over, Cheshire would switch from his Mosquito to a borrowed American P-51 Mustang, an exceedingly fast and powerful fighter that he took on a marking mission the day he received it, despite having no previous combat experience flying a single-seater and navigating by himself. This same strong individualism characterizes Air Vice-Marshal Don Bennett, the self-styled "leader of the Pathfinders," who developed this target-marking force against great opposition both from the German defenses and from elements of the RAF unappreciative of his self-driven spirit. Even today the opinion of memoirists is divided about Bennett; some give him credit and hail his success, others ascribe the idea for the Pathfinders to the Air Ministry's Sidney Bufton and Ivelaw Chapman or question the Pathfinders' true worth. Even their importance as an alternative to the immorality of indiscriminate bombing is a matter for debate. Don Charlwood's *No Moon Tonight* concludes with an old friend from training days regretting the size and momentum of the bomber offensive: "I suppose it will go on until all the beauty and culture are bombed out of Europe" (p. 173). He elects a tour with the Pathfinders as an antidote, for the precision of their marking lessens the charge of random slaughter. But

Walter Thompson's *Lancaster to Berlin* tells a different story, one of a pilot dedicated to bombing only military targets who regrets releasing his ordnance on the abstraction of a Pathfinder flare over a target he himself cannot see, especially since in the past, flying low, he has seen the Pathfinders misidentify objectives. But the Pathfinders, developed in mid 1942 and established as an independent Group by the start of 1943, had the course of the air war on their side; when the Germans developed the ability to jam the Gee radar guidance system, the Pathfinders became Bomber Command's only effective eyes.

A big reason for the debate is the personality of Don Bennett himself. His memoir, *Pathfinder,* bristles with political rancor, and any fellow memoirist asking him for a foreword (whether the appreciative Charlwood or the more critical Thompson) risks unleashing even more invective and recrimination. Yet Bennett's most prominent quality, from which these political irritations may derive, is intense individualism. He is always best in man-to-man situations, and having first served under Sir Arthur Harris in a flying boat squadron in 1932, ten years later he welcomes his old leader's ascension to Bomber Command. Harris, he notes approvingly, "was full of fire and dash, was not easily balked, and was also remarkably intelligent without trying to show it. He was, I knew, a real man, and my hopes for the bomber offensive and its ultimate destruction of Germany were revitalized" (p. 141). Harris's own view of Bennett, ventured in 1947 while both principals were still quite active on the scene, is more tempered:

> His courage, both moral and physical, is outstanding, and as a technician he is unrivalled. He will forgive me if I say that his consciousness of his own intellectual powers sometimes made him impatient with slower or differently constituted minds, so that some people found him difficult to work with. He could not suffer fools gladly, and by his own high standards there were many fools. (pp. 129–30)

Bennett took delight in his bull-headed freedom. Bader might phone Group Commanders at midnight and argue his case to the highest levels of government, but Bennett preferred actions to words: when the Air Ministry was slow to remove an old rifle range building obstructing a runway at Wyton, Bennett bombed his own airfield and removed the offending structure with a direct hit by a 250-pounder. When told Mosquitoes could not operate in darkness, he replied that he had been flying one at night for weeks with no trouble at all.

Having piloted an American B-25 in conditions of zero visibility at night, he enjoyed answering whether he had ever seen a Mitchell bomber with the quip that although he had never *seen* one, he had flown one.

Bennett's thinking reflects that of Harris when he points out that "the bombing of a German target on one single occasion was the equivalent of going through the Battle of Jutland or any other great battle" (Bennett, p. 138) and that bomber crews were expected to do this night after night no less than thirty times before their tour was complete and they had earned a half-year's rest as instructors. Bennett's twist was that such massive war power deserved better guidance than merely sending novice pilots and ill-equipped navigators out two hundred to six hundred miles in the dark, where clouds often prevented astral sightings and the ground was obscured by blackouts. Why not, he wondered, put the very best men with the finest equipment in a few lead planes and trust them to mark targets for the rest? Such individualism struck directly against the Bomber Command style of crew solidarity and, to some extent, anonymity. Even on a larger organizational level few Group or Squadron commanders liked having their best people stolen from the ranks, and one Group with a good reputation for accuracy—Ralph Cochrane's 5 Group—resented Bennett's theft of their talent. Radar equipment became the Pathfinders' wizardry, first with H2S units, which distinguished ground features, and then with Oboe, a method by which two signals converge on the target (unlike Gee, Oboe's broadcast band was too narrow and discriminative to jam). But with visual methods alone Bennett's force established an effective procedure for finding and marking objectives:

> We first put in what we call Finders, with some Supporters at exactly the same time. These Finders were generally at about zero minus five minutes, and they were the best crews available. They had a good load of flares, which they dropped at the point or points where they thought the aiming point was to be found. One or other of these experts would in due course put a bunch of flares over the correct aiming point, and having identified it would then drop further flares on top of it. As soon as this had taken place, the Illuminators would come in, and would put a stick of flares across the aiming point as found by the Finders. After the Illuminators came the Primary Markers, who were accurate bomb aimers, and who dropped target indicators on the aiming point as identified visually in the excellent light of the sticks of flares. Once the aiming point was marked, we then

followed up with Backers-Up, who put further target indicators
on the mark previously made so that the Main Force had a mark
at which to continue to aim throughout the duration of the attack. (pp. 185–86)

Targets could be marked on the ground visually or by H2S, or above
the clouds with sky markers. The entire system was complex yet flexi-
ble, unlike the Luftwaffe's 1940–41 technique of "fire lighting," which
used electronics to guide to the target special bombers, whose crews
simply dropped incendiaries to serve as signal fires for the force to
follow. Bennett's Pathfinders used color-coded flares, the combina-
tions of which were changed daily so that dummy fires and faked
target indicators would distract no one. Bennett dismissed out of
hand Cheshire's style of low-altitude marking, feeling that ground
speed was too high for accurate release and that even broken cloud
cover would obscure these small markers from the bombers ten to
twenty thousand feet above.

The dam busters and Pathfinders provide both strategies and
heroes because their tasks are sufficiently small and specific to grasp.
The overall size of the bomber offensive, however, defies the imagination; it has few individual heroes or striking metaphors, just an immensity of numbers and destruction. In 1942, when Harris felt he had
to work like a traveling salesman promoting his product to the Air
Ministry, he felt it necessary to deal in the apocalyptic sum of thou-
sand-bomber raids against Cologne and the Ruhr—nine hundred
ninety-nine bombers would not do—and so training units had to be
scoured in search of serviceable planes and minimally competent
crews to reach the magic, prophetic whole. Attrition was ghastly;
Bomber Command lost and replaced as many as eight hundred
heavies in one 4-month period and counted nearly fifty thousand fatal
casualties—three-quarters of their total flying force—during the war.
Over one million Germans were directly involved in the air defense of
the Reich, and antiaircraft guns retained to defend their cities meant
fewer antitank weapons on the Eastern front. Memoirists on both
sides note that when the United States entered the war with plans to
build forty-seven thousand bombers per year, the tide had inevitably
turned. By the end of *Bomber Offensive* Sir Arthur Harris is able to
tick off the hundreds of thousands of acres destroyed within Germany's cities, numbers that swamp our ability to comprehend.

The most sensitive of Bomber Command memoirists find themselves swept up in these numbers. In *No Moon Tonight* Don

Charlwood begins with the fear that completing thirty missions will be impossible; all around him crews are failing to return from their fifth, tenth, or twentieth raid, and the men who can count just a few operations left are rare. But as he and his comrades pass the midpoint, a sense of confidence sets in, and by the time of their last missions he is consciously wishing for more of them, so dependable has the crew-oriented routine become. The repetition of these patterns, thirty times over half a year or more and perhaps again through a second tour, makes bomber service a life in itself. As Charlwood ends his book with his wartime romance passing into memory, his crew dispersing, and the airfield at Elsham Wolds disappearing behind him in the fog, he cannot believe his own words—"Surely not, Never again! Surely not, Never!" (p. 178)—for the experience has transformed his life and left nothing to replace it.

Walter Thompson's *Lancaster to Berlin* is built on the more consciously moral problem of dedication to bombing only military targets. This freedom of choice is steadily compromised in small steps that not even the most scrupulous person could debate, until by the end it is all-out bitter war. "There was no longer any feeling in Bomber Command that we were attacking industrial targets," Thompson concludes. "We were desperately trying to win a war with air power alone" (p. 131). Along the way memoirists note occasional points of humor—dropping packages of tea on austerely suffering Holland and being thanked by Dutchmen years later—and are grateful when they can recount examples of remarkable providence, such as one crew member bailing out without his parachute but landing safely in a snowbank, his fall broken by a huge pine; another whose chute fails before he comes to rest atop the canopy of another falling below him; the story of a tail gunner who fails to hear the call to abandon ship and innocently rides the plane down to a survivable crash, and whose critique of the pilot's bumpy landing stops short when he finds the cockpit and the rest of the plane totally deserted. But the tide toward total war envelops all of these narratives, just as the bombers no sooner cross the enemy coast than, one by one, they catch a burst of flak or night fighter fire and fall away to earth.

The devastation wrought by Bomber Command strikes even its advocates as an assault upon nature, and the best descriptions of this offensive are rich with weirdly unnatural details. The destruction of Hamburg, regarded by strategists as the bombers' greatest success, awes pilot Walter Thompson, who can see smoke from the city rising twenty thousand feet into the air and can spot its fires from over one hundred miles away, even as he flies to restoke them. The final attack, on the night of August 2, 1943, takes place in a wicked electrical storm, the elements themselves striving to outdo Bomber Command's spectacle of destruction:

> Towering cumulo-nimbus clouds were all around us. One wouldn't have seen them in the dark, except for the massive and violent lightning strikes. St. Elmo's fire shot blue sparks across the windscreen and instrument panel and blue flames circled around the four whirling propellors and off the gun barrels. Lightning struck our aircraft twice. At one point huge blue balls of static electricity, two feet in diameter, headed down the fuse-lage beside me, presumably to run out of the training aerials. When approaching Hamburg a dazzling display of lightning lit up two clouds directly ahead of us and between them a Lancaster was flying. I saw a flash of what appeared to be lightning across the gap between the two clouds and then was shocked to see the Lancaster blow up in an orange and black ball of flame. Whether it was hit by flak or whether the lightning had caused a fire I was not sure, because a white flash preceded the orange ball. (pp. 129–30)

The Hamburg raids, during which the RAF discovered that constantly rekindled fires would create a fire storm of 200-mile per hour winds capable of melting pavement and asphixiating people even deep below ground in shelters, set the style for destruction from then on. The climax of the bomber war against cities was the controversial Dresden raid on February 13, 1945, which caused between 130,000 and 250,000 deaths and ranks as the largest one-day massacre in European history. Following this Bomber Command was considering a 3,000-bomber raid against Berlin as a demonstration of overwhelming Allied might. But by then the armies were advancing so rapidly that bombers were no longer needed. The greatest offensive campaign in the history of warfare had come to a close.

The aftermath of Bomber Command's war is ambiguous. Harris was denied the peerage his fellow commanders received, and his crews won no campaign medals. Postwar surveys by the Americans debated many of Harris's claims for the breadth and effectiveness of Bomber Command, and the Dresden raid prompted charges of atrocity and political mismanagement. Even the postwar careers of the dam buster and Pathfinder heroes, the only bomber pilots widely known, are odd affairs. Don Bennett became a political irascible, serving in Parliament and as the chairman of committees to remove Britain from the Common Market and strengthen military power. Leonard Cheshire took the opposite path to charity and pacifism, preaching Christianity from a fleet of traveling bus exhibits and founding several homes for the chronically ill. Each man considered his calling to be a direct response to the lessons taught by the war.

What of the common fliers? Their memoirs are among the most touching of the war, both because of the dangers they faced and the great vacuum they felt as the war ended and their stature, like their targets, crumbled into ruins. At the close of *No Moon Tonight* Don Charlwood is a lost man, and Jack Currie concludes *Mosquito Victory* by declining to enter Lincoln Cathedral, preferring to keep it as the landmark it has been for the past three years of his life. In Geoff Taylor's *Piece of Cake* two and a half years are compressed into one long day, but even before his prisoner-of-war experience begins he notes how for a Lancaster pilot the rhythms and cycles of nature are reversed:

> It was like looking at the outside world through the wrong end of a telescope. Nature had only been apparent as a dirty night or a good night for flying. It was the moon, the German nightfighter's moon, that we thought about most. The moon it was, in all its phases, that governed the tide and tempo of our flying. Sunset had become the evening symbol of the beginning of one's personal share in the war. The dawn had become the best part of the day. Triumphant over the fenland mists that could shroud a flarepath while your back was turned on the downward leg of the circuit, the dawn was a thing to warm your bones. You associated it with the incessant roar of engines spluttering and backfiring into a silence so peaceful and positive that it left you drowsy with the relaxation of strain and concentration; so drowsy that it took actual physical effort to slip off your sweaty helmet, slide back the altitude-chilled panel in the cockpit canopy and lean out to feel the fresh air on your face and welcome the pleasurable sounds and sights of earth. (p. 2)

When comparing their roles with those of fighter pilots, Harris's bomber boys had many things to consider, but paramount was the enormity of their enemy—not the German defenses or the limits of gravity and of their own equipment, but of nature itself, whose clock they reversed and whose dark and quiet night they turned into a raging inferno. Walter Thompson, upon meeting Buzz Beurling, the ace fighter pilot of Malta who flew against the most incredible odds of the war, accepts the hero's admission that the bomber pilot's job is harder. They go on to compare philosophies, based on Richthofen's belief that to succeed one must never consider oneself a potential victim, that it must always be the enemy who will fall. This did not hold true in the bomber war, Thompson maintains. "Something more was required," he advises his new friend. "One had to learn to accept death and become used to the idea of it. One had to consider oneself as already dead" (p. 103).

6

Adversaries

A German pilot, helped from the wreckage of his Junkers 88 bomber, tells his British captors that he does speak English, having read Law at Merton College, Oxford, before the war. Another Luftwaffe crewman is brought down in Richmond, where he had lived for several years in the 1930s. On the RAF side, nearly every memoirist can tell of some experience in prewar Germany. Richard Hillary rowed crew for General Göring's own Prize Fours; Leonard Cheshire lived for part of a year with an increasingly Nazified family in Potsdam; C. F. Rawnsley and his wife spent the midsummer holiday of Sonnwenfeuer in the little village of Kaub on the Rhine, only to have this idyll interrupted by a militaristic torchlight parade. A contingent of Luftwaffe generals visited the Hendon Air Display, and into the late 1930s Germany and Great Britain exchanged equipment, with a Heinkel fighter airframe serving as the test-bed for British engines, which were in turn used to power the initial Messerschmitt prototypes. While English servicemen spent their leaves in a France soon to be hostile occupied territory, Lufthansa pilots on the Berlin-London airline route mapped future bombing runs.

It is air power that brings these two nations close together, whether it be the short flight to each other's capitals or the comradely spirit among their airmen. Although the Luftwaffe was the most politicized of the German military services, and the RAF boasted the most ideal commitment to its country's war aims (and were so credited in Prime Minister Churchill's speeches), the wartime meeting of these foes produced something other than a simple fight to the death. What distinguishes these fliers' spirit in combat also influences the style of their narratives in its aftermath.

The fliers of one country recognize their opponents' professionalism. In the first words of *Wing Leader* Johnnie Johnson remarks that as the war ended his wing was engaging the Luftwaffe almost every day, "and although they were in a hopeless position, short of fuel and spares and their airfields under constant bombardment, let it be said to their credit that they continued to fight until the end" (p. 1). In *Duel of Eagles* Peter Townsend thinks as much about his German counterparts as he does about himself and the RAF. He parallels the two services' histories and takes pains to find out who exactly his opponents were, what they had been doing the day he shot them down, and how his and their lives had proceeded on similar tracks all the years from childhood and school to this moment in 1940 when they met in battle. Bob Braham makes this same sympathetic identification in *"Scramble!"*. As the victorious pilot rummages through the wreckage of his kill for a souvenir, he "unearths some gruesome remains—part of the leg of one of the German crew," and for the first time he sees there is another side to this story:

> Up to this stage I hadn't really thought in terms of killing individuals. Air combat to me was an impersonal thing, one machine against another, with none of the unpleasantness of close combat land warfare. But after seeing the wreck of this German plane, I couldn't help feeling some remorse for the enemy crew who, though enemies, were fighting like us for their country. They would be mourned in their homeland like any of our lads who had fallen. (p. 61)

German memoirs speak with the same understanding. Introducing Heinz Knoke's *I Flew for the Führer*, General E. R. Quesada of the U.S. Air Force comments that the author "was a fine airman, very brave, and an excellent pilot. I would have liked having him in one of my own squadrons" (p. v). Knoke himself admires not only the RAF's equipment (he takes special pride in being able to shoot down the challenging Spitfire) but also the spirit of its pilot, whom he finds to be "tough, but a clean fighter. The story of the achievements of the British fighter pilots will always remain a glorious chapter in the history of air warfare" (p. 32). He is moved by the courage of the Swordfish pilots who attacked the German cruisers in the Channel, none of whom survived. And when Knoke receives the German Gold Cross from Hermann Göring, the Reichsmarshal commends the RAF for its bravery as well. Hitler hears Adolf Galland's objections to the German journalists and broadcasters who defame the enemy and agrees that the slanders must stop; their foes are not to be discussed "in a condescending or presumptuous tone," nor are their achievements to be denigrated (p. 45).

The greatest enemy, writers on both sides soon learn, is the abstractness that often frames their combat in unreal terms. This becomes hardest for the bomber crews, removed as they are from the immediate effects of their actions. In *No Moon Tonight* navigator Don Charlwood is aware of this contradiction even as he plots his course home: "I fasten my blackout curtain and turn up the Anglepoise lamp. The outer scene becomes something unreal; the real world is this glaring chart with its bare outline of coasts and rivers. The Gee indicates that we are approaching [their station at] Elsham, not the Elsham of the mess and barracks, but an Elsham that is a spot of ink on the chart before me" (p. 111). In *Lancaster Target* pilot Jack Currie expresses the same sentiment, this time as a safeguard against crippling guilt:

> As the bombs fell, the fact that I should feel no shock of personal reaction was itself a sort of shock. Perhaps it was an act of such incalculable violence as to prohibit normal comprehension. My small experience of previous, and far less violent acts had taught me that they bred a sense of guilty self-dislike. So what appalling pang might be aroused by this atrocious deed? But that hollow in my mind remained unfilled, and the need to concentrate on height and speed and heading took command of all my thoughts.
>
> We hung, balanced and steady, in the midst of an expanse of flame-shot havoc. Certainly, the enemy was doing his utmost to destroy us in his turn, to find us with radar and searchlights, to kill us with bullets from his fighters and shells from his guns. That was a physical matter for us, and would be physically resolved. What could not be resolved was the gross imbalance of the scene: the contrast of the bright chaos that seethed four miles below us with the cold, pale readings on my cockpit dials, the flat laconic comments of the crew. (p. 44)

As for the bomb aimer, Larry Myring, Currie guesses that it is best that "no picture came into his mind of shattered limbs, of burning clothing, of living bodies crushed by rubble" (p. 72). He too takes refuge in his equipment, thumbing the release button as the target indicator appears within his bombsight. "Maybe I had greater imaginative resources," Currie speculates, "but at such times they seemed to be switched off. My mind was just as closed as Larry's; as I held the aircraft steady for his aim I saw no bloody pictures, had no memories of what I'd seen in London in the blitz" (pp. 72–73). Even the crewman's designation bespeaks an abstract action: he is not a bombardier but a bomb aimer, as if what happens after he takes aim is someone else's business.

On the ground RAF airmen are no different, finding it much easier to identify with their Luftwaffe counterparts overhead than with their fellow Britons who are suffering the bombing, so abstracted are these fliers within their roles. Similarly, in air battles the fighter pilot completes his kill and only then gives thought to his victims inside the plane; their presence now adds power to the description, whereas before they would have retarded it. Consider Peter Townsend's pacing of the action in *Duel of Eagles:*

> The effect of my guns was devastating. The bomber staggered, emitting a cloud of oily vapor that obscured my windscreen. Then, as if the pilot had collapsed over the controls, it tipped into a steep dive at a terrifying speed. Suddenly both wings were wrenched off with a fearful violence and the dismembered fuselage plummeted straight into the sea, followed by a trail of fluttering debris. Only at that moment did I realize what I had done to the men inside. I felt utterly nauseated. (p. 210)

For most of the paragraph Townsend focuses on the bomber, so vital a thing that it takes on living qualities ("staggered," "fluttering"). The enemy pilot is first mentioned only in relation to the aircraft's controls and behavior, and the fate of the crew provides a fitting climax to all this destruction.

Other times Townsend will follow a victim down to the sea, where the German crewmen become "no longer enemies but airmen in distress" and he can wish that "we could have borne up their doomed aircraft with our own wings" (p. 214), another personification of equipment. He tells of a colleague who intends to keep some fragments from a wrecked kill until he examines the dead pilot's wallet and finds photos of his wife and letters from her; only then does he "realize what he had done" (p. 316). (Guy Gibson's own rummaging for souvenirs is tempered by his intention to return his dead foe's Iron Cross to the man's family in Germany.) This ability to abstract the human and concentrate on equipment, at least until the engagement is over and there is time for sympathy, Townsend retains until near the end of his memoir, when the fury of the Battle of Britain mounts to the point that "both life and death had lost their importance. Desire had sharpened to a single savage purpose—to grab the enemy and claw him down from the sky" (p. 374)—but even here the writer attributes his newly hostile feeling to fatigue.

In Wilhelm Johnen's narration of his kills in *Duel Under the Stars* all expression of sympathy for the victims is withheld until after a description of the mechanical action, which concludes with the ample pyrotechnics of bombers bursting into flame and crashing into pools of fire on the ground. It is the strength of German air defenses in the Ruhr that makes this night fighter pilot pity the bomber crews who must fly through it. His greatest regret is for the hapless gunner who bails out directly into his path; when the Messerschmitt 110 lands there are traces of blood and hair on the propellers and strips of uniform hang from the radar antenna—another example of equipment consuming a man. Yet Johnen can see his own cities burning, and like Currie he confesses that "the bomber must be brought down at all costs, and when it crashes we crow. We only see the bomber burning and not the crew. We only see the emblem laid low, not the youngsters hanging on their straps in their death agony" (pp. 82–83).

When face-to-face meetings are inescapable, another style takes over, replacing abstract technique with acts of chivalry. High-ranking commanders on both sides—Göring and Udet, Dowding and Douglas—were World War I fliers, and all had traditions of gentlemanly behavior to uphold. Ernst Udet liked to tell of how the French ace Georges Guynemer had inverted his plane, waved, and flown away when he found that his German foe's guns were jammed, and Udet refused to believe that it was merely a case of the Frenchman's weapon also malfunctioning. Between the wars Udet worked as a barnstormer and aerial filmmaker. In 1930 he went missing in the Sudan; his old enemy Sholto Douglas, however, was in command at Khartoum, and he both arranged for Udet's rescue and entertained him afterward. Most World War II pilots practice and experience the same chivalry and record instances of it fondly. When Bob Braham and his navigator are shot down over Denmark, they flee their plane certain that the predator Focke-Wulfs will strafe them. "There was no shelter and we couldn't run," Braham recalls. "We just stood still and hoped. As they roared over us at twenty or so feet the leader, whose helmeted head I could clearly see, waved. I waved back, and as they winged away to their base I thought what chivalrous foes they had been" (p. 23). The Luftwaffe pilot, Leutnant Robert Spreckels, soon visits the imprisoned British flier, expresses pleasure at his survival, and lays the groundwork for a postwar friendship that culminates in his introducing Braham's own memoirs.

A similar episode takes place over Elham valley as the Battle of Britain concludes in October 1940. Flying Officer Eric Thomas of 222 Squadron pursues a Messerschmitt 109 piloted by Feldwebel Fritz Schweser and brings it down with a lucky shot into its oil radiator. Streaming smoke and oil, the German fighter seizes up and glides toward an open field, a scene the village vicar records in Dennis Knight's *Harvest of Messerschmitts*:

> Last month I watched a British airman force down a German fighter plane on the outskirts of the parish. The Englishman was merciful, as it seemed to me. He could have blown to pieces the German pilot, but he withheld his fire when the Nazi was obviously beaten and coming down. He afterwards circled around for some time to make sure of his "bag," and then did something which fairly took my breath away—he quickly rolled his plane over in the air, as you might spin a tennis racket in your hand! It is, I believe, what the RAF call "The Victory Roll." (p. 147)

The Spitfire's roll, of course, is a standard image in the iconography of the Battle of Britain and of the RAF's air war in general. But how pure is that image when contemplated in the context of one airman having spared an enemy's life, no small consideration to the man of God telling this story? The comparisons to tennis, the hunter's bag, and fairly beating one's opponent reenforce the good sport nature of the whole affair.

Such courtesy at times extends to foes still in the air. In Peter Townsend's *Duel of Eagles* Stuka pilot Rudolf Braun tells how, with his dive breaks jammed after an attack, he limped out to sea surrounded by Hurricanes and Spitfires: " 'I saw fighters all around me who knew I was winged. They passed me to right and left and above me. Incredibly, they did not shoot, but only waved' " (p. 346). As in Udet's encounter with Guynemer, this may have been a case of fighters returning from engagements with their ammunition spent, but it is nice for memoirists on both sides to assume, as did Udet, that a better aspect of human nature was showing through.

Indeed, human nature has ample opportunity to show itself at its best in these memoirs. After several RAF planes are lost over the Bay of Biscay when their position was reported to the Luftwaffe by supposedly neutral Spanish fishing boats, the ever excitable Bob Braham resolves to take his Beaufighter on a strafing mission against these vessels. Stung by the loss of his colleagues and eager for revenge, he swoops down, lines up a boat in his sights, and prepares to fire. But at the last moment he sees a child, most likely the son of the boat's owner, guilelessly waving hello. The startled pilot calls off his attack and returns to base. "With that my anger against the treachery of these supposed neutrals left me," he confides. "Even though some of them might have been responsible for the death of my two crews, I couldn't commit murder" (p. 121). Later he faces a similar temptation when a Messerschmitt 110, after nearly colliding with him in midair, explodes directly in front of him. Braham and his crewmate are not injured, but the impetuous pilot is so shaken that at the sight of a floating parachute he resolves to "finish him off." His AI operator dissuades him—with some irony, as the operator is Jewish and news of the death camps has just begun to leak out. Braham wishes he could call out to the dangling German airman that one of his country's persecuted has saved him.

The issue of firing at men in parachutes offers fliers the chance to place chivalry ahead of situational ethics. The Geneva Convention speaks to them too abstractly: if an airman bails out over enemy territory, the Convention explains, his life is to be spared, for it is expected that he will be interned for the duration of the war as a prisoner and hence will be safely *hors de combat*. But if a flier is parachuting over his own country, it must be assumed he will be returning to combat; therefore most RAF pilots shot down during the Battle of Britain became fair game for Messerschmitt guns. In practice, no memoirist admits to gunning down such a helpless opponent (though Bob Braham evokes tension by flirting with the idea). When an occasional Hurricane or Spitfire pilot is machine-gunned in his parachute over Sussex or Kent, the RAF writer does not complain about its tactical unfairness but warns that this one kill will cost the Germans more in the long run, thanks to the greater aggressiveness among RAF pilots that these pathetic losses inspire. Such is the feeling Tom Gleave expresses in *I Had a Row With a German*. Gleave was shot down during the Battle of Britain and writes while Great Britain is still fighting at a disadvantage. In *Lancaster Target* Jack Currie records surprise and outrage at the murder of British crewmen in parachutes over Germany until a colleague puts it in perspective:

> I had no strong views about the pilots of the night-fighters who opposed us in the campaign over Germany, and certainly no antipathy, until the night I saw a bomber crew bale out over the

western suburbs of Berlin, and the pilot of an Me109 fired burst after burst of gunfire at the figures swinging helplessly below their parachutes. First I felt sickened at the scene, silhouetted against the fires and smoke below, then I grew hot with anger at the bloody, vengeful act. I mentioned the incident later in the flight office, and said that I now took a harsher view of German pilots.

"I'm finished with all that balls about the Jerry pilots being just like us. I couldn't have shot those parachutes up."

The Gunnery Leader shrugged, and commented:

"He may have been a Berliner himself, and he might have lost a wife, or his favorite popsy, in a raid last week. You never know."

"Okay, and so have some of our chaps lost relatives in the blitz, but it hasn't turned them into murderous bastards, like that fellow."

"How do you know it hasn't? It's a murderous bloody war, old mate." (p. 159)

The image Currie sustains is that of airmen who do not file away their feelings with their flight plans; they are outraged to see fliers being slaughtered yet, like Braham, are tempted to do it themselves. They resolve the problem by having these emotions put into perspective by a comrade. That the memoirists are attempting to keep a British image intact becomes clear in Dennis Knight's *Harvest of Messerschmitts,* when the squadrons accused of "queuing up" to shoot a falling German airman are identified as expatriate Poles. More common is Johnnie Johnson's warning to his wing that any pilot seen shooting an enemy in parachute will be court-martialed.

British and German memoirs contain far more examples of enemy airmen helping each other. Tom Gleave points out how many downed Luftwaffe fliers, otherwise sure to drown, are rescued by Royal Navy launches, and Wilhem Johnen cites the following order from his commander: "Naturally you have to help the enemy if he should fall into the drink" (p. 97). In *Fighter* Len Deighton quotes a story told by Messerschmitt pilot Erich Rudorffer (who ended the war as a top German ace with over two hundred victories) about the lack of bitterness that characterized even the hardest fighting:

"Once—I think it was 31 August 1940—I was in a fight with four Hurricanes over Dover. I was back over the Channel when I saw another Hurricane coming from Calais, trailing white smoke, obviously in a bad way. I flew up alongside him and escorted him all the way to England and then waved goodbye. A few weeks later the same thing happened to me. That would never have happened in Russia—never." (p. 251)

When opposing airmen meet face to face once the shooting is done, a spirit of help and cooperation prevails. Bob Braham is introduced to Robert Spreckels, the Focke-Wulf 190 pilot who downed his plane but refused to strafe its wreckage, and takes an immediate liking to his foe. This feeling is reinforced when he learns the German's parents died in the massive bombing of Hamburg, a catastrophe that would have provoked lesser men to savage their enemies without quarter. Braham's reaction to the meeting is typical; he writes that Spreckels "seemed so frank and friendly and in many ways like so many of my friends in the RAF" (p. 198). This feeling of common understanding eclipses even politics. A German interrogation officer suggests that Braham join him in fighting against Russia but almost at once hesitates when he realizes that the British pilot would do just as he would—take the controls of the plane and head for home.

This is precisely the scene when two of the war's top fighter pilots, Douglas Bader and Adolf Galland, meet after Bader is brought down over France. Galland offers a tour of the airfield, and Bader asks if he can sit in the cockpit of Galland's Messerschmitt 109:

> "Why not!" Everything had to be explained to him in the smallest detail. I enjoyed the interest and understanding this great pilot showed. He would have fitted splendidly into our "club."
>
> Bader bent down to me from the cockpit of my plane in which he still sat and said, "Will you do me a great favor?"
>
> "With pleasure, if it is in my power," I answered.
>
> "At least once in my life I would like to fly a Messerschmitt. Let me do just one circle over the airfield." He said it with a smile and looked me straight in the eyes. I nearly weakened.
>
> But I said, "If I grant you your wish, I'm afraid you'll escape and I should be forced to chase after you. Now we have met we don't want to shoot at each other again, do we!" He laughed and we changed the subject. After a hearty good-by he went back to the hospital. (Galland, *The First and the Last*, pp. 90–91)

Paul Brickhill's replay of this scene in *Reach for the Sky* is even more colorful than Galland's, although in Brickhill's version the two men speak through an interpreter:

Bader looked at it [the Messerschmitt 109] fascinated, and Galland made a polite gesture for him to climb in. He surprised them by the way he hauled himself on to the wing-root, grabbed his right leg and swung it into the cockpit and climbed in un-aided. As he cast a glinting professional eye over the cockpit lay-out Galland leaned in and pointed things out. Mad thoughts about starting up and slamming the throttle on for a reckless take-off surged through Bader's mind.

Lifting his head, he could see no signs of the aerodrome. He turned to the interpreter. "Would you ask the Herr Oberstleut-nant if I can take off and try a little trip in this thing?"

Galland chuckled and answered. The interpreter grinned at Bader. "He says that if you do he'll be taking off right after you."

"All right," Bader said, looking a little too eagerly at Gal-land. "Let's have a go."

Galland chuckled again and said that he was off duty at the moment. (pp. 293–94)

Each flier recasts the scene to admire his opponent's skill in both aeronautics and rhetoric, yet remains personally in control. Bader's mind may well be set on the white cliffs of Dover, but a photograph in the book clarifies the reality of the moment for the reader: just behind the two airmen stands a German officer with a Luger pistol at ready.

Poetic justice and narrative form would have profited from hav-ing Galland himself be the pilot who shot down Bader; as it was, there had to be some tampering with squadron records at the RAF ace's behest so that it would appear he was bested by a German officer and not just a noncom. Such actual face-to-face dramas did take place, not between the war's glamorous heroes, though, but among the lower ranks who did most of the fighting yet who maintained the same idealism as their superior officers when dealing with captured foes. Consider the remarkable scene in *I Flew for the Führer* when Heinz Knoke's irreparably damaged Messerschmitt manages to bring down the attacking P-47 Thunderbolt before both planes fall to earth within a few hundred yards of one another:

When I next recover consciousness, I become aware of a man standing motionless and staring down at me. He is as tall as a young tree—an American!

I try to sit up on the edge of the ditch. The big fellow sits down beside me. At first neither of us speak. It is all I can do to prop my elbows on my knees and hold my splitting head in my hands. Then the Yank offers me a cigarette. I thank him and refuse, at the same time offering him one of mine. He also refuses; so we both light up our own.

"Was that you flying the Messerschmitt?"

"Yes," I answer in my rusty English.

"You wounded?"

"Feels like it."

"The back of your head is bleeding."

I can feel the blood trickling down my neck.

The Yank continues. "Did you really shoot me down?"

"Yes."

"But I don't see how you could! Your kite was a mass of flames."

"Don't I know it!" (p. 179)

This languid postcoital conversation over cigarettes continues, and the frenzy of combat yields to an easy replay of tactics and to admiration for each other's skill, including scores: " 'Guess I'm not the first you bagged, am I?' 'No; you are my twenty-sixth' " (p. 179). From here the talk turns to personal facts; the German learns that the American was due to return home in a few days, and the American notices the German's wedding ring and is then shown pictures of his wife and children. "We have a friendly chat for about half an hour," Knoke concludes. "He seems like a decent fellow. There is no suggestion of hatred between us, nor any reason for it. We have too much in common. We are both pilots, and we have both just narrowly escaped death" (p. 180).

Erich Rudorffer had maintained that such decency was a Western phenomenon impossible on the Russian front. But when Wilhelm Johnen must bring down a Russian transport he admits to feeling "sorry for the crew" and fires at the wingtips so that "if the machine crashed the crew would be able to be saved"; yet only one man bails out. The next day Johnen visits him in the hospital and learns the sad truth: the plane had carried young cadets, all without parachutes. With tears in his eyes the pilot absolves the shaken Johnen: "You meant well, comrade" (p. 175).

Legends of the more famous fliers precede them into combat. It is touching to read of the German physician who, when drawing back Bader's bedcovers to see for the first time his missing legs, remarks, "We have heard of you"; or to read of Pierre Closterman's squadron mourning the death of Luftwaffe ace Walter Nowotny. The German flier is remembered with respect and even affection, which impresses

Closterman; for the first time he sees that there is indeed a solidarity among pilots "which is above all tragedies and all prejudices" (*The Big Show*, p. 170). The timing here is significant: Closterman and his colleagues have switched from nimble Spitfires to larger, more powerful Typhoons, and have been undertaking those ground attack duties so unpleasant to the true fighter pilot. It is November 8, 1944; the Allies are well established in France and the Reich is beginning to crumble under the heavy bombardment that resumed once Bomber Command was released from General Eisenhower's control. Nowotny's death was heroic, as he disregarded his own grounding to lead a flight of Messerschmitt 262 jets—the Luftwaffe's last, fatally delayed hope—against the continuous onslaught of American bombers. He brought one down, his 258th kill, but lost an engine in the process. His return to base was frustrated by a group of P-51 Mustangs "hunting the crippled Me262 like a pack of hounds" (p. 361), as Hans Dieter Berenbrok reports in *The Luftwaffe Diaries*. Prevented from landing, Nowotny had no choice but to fight it out, which cost him his life at age twenty-three. Yet after what Closterman has been experiencing on the ground, the German's death seems noble and reminds him of how pure and unsullied the air had been:

> This war has witnessed appalling massacres, towns crushed by bombs, the butchery of Oradour, the ruins of Hamburg. We ourselves had been sickened when our shells exploded in a peaceful village street, mowing down women and children round the German tank we were attacking. In comparison our tussles with Nowotny and his Messerschmitts were something clean, above the fighting on the ground, in the mud and the blood, in the deafening din of the crawling, stinking tanks. (Closterman, pp. 170–71)

Such reverence for a fallen enemy is in fact part of a flier's own self-esteem and is needed to maintain the image he has of "Dog-fights in the sky: silvery midges dancing in graceful arabesques—the diaphanous tracery of milky condensation trails—Focke-Wulfs skimming like toys in the infinite sky" (p. 171), all of which Closterman sees ending with his transfer to tactical duties and with the close of the war itself. His description of their attacks against trains is equally graphic but is couched in repulsive terms, the grim reality of war asserting itself as war. "We could rise above all this to-day by saluting a brave enemy who had just died, by saying that Nowotny belonged to us, that he was part of our world, where there were no ideologies, no hatred and no frontiers." There is even time for the loftiest (and most impractical) sentiment of all: "Whoever first dared paint markings on a plane's wing was a swine!" (p. 171), the same sense of blasphemy Peter Townsend felt during the Munich crisis when ordered to camouflage his silver Hawker Fury in the grim paint of war.

The ideal of the "clean fight" motivates nearly all memoirists' descriptions of meeting their foes in the air. Tony Dudgeon's first such engagement of the war, which he details in *The Luck of the Devil*, comes during a bombing mission in his Blenheim against El Adem, when an Italian fighter shadows him for so long that his ire is raised and he decides to trick his pursuer with some cloud-hopping out to sea into a headwind sure to exhaust the fighter's fuel. The ploy works, and the Italian airman, once drawn beyond his range, drops into the Mediterranean as his tardy quest for home falls short:

> I waited for his helmeted head to appear beside the sinking fuselage as I circled the spot. I told Bennett to get the rubber dinghy pack ready to drop through the rear hatch. We realized that in the southerly wind his only hope would be for the dinghy to be blown the 200 miles north to Crete. His machine sank lower, and lower, and then I realized that he was not going to appear. I felt awful. It stopped being, as I sensed earlier, a clean fight with an enemy, and let the best man win. That he would have killed me, if he could, counted for nothing. I had capitalized directly on his enthusiasm, inexperience and, probably, youth. I had tricked a youngster, another pilot, into committing suicide. It was a terrible feeling and my flight back to base was a misery. (p. 154)

The single "dirty kill" comes at the hand of renegade hero Buzz Beurling, who at the time already was established as the black sheep of the RAF and who eventually was eased out of the service despite his great success. It is indicative of his manner that he characterizes enemies as "screwballs" and makes his kills as bloody as possible — at least in their telling. His most notorious kill involves stalking an open-cockpit Italian fighter and taking aim at the pilot's head, which explodes in a burst of cannon fire, leaving the poor man's severed artery to pump blood across the aircraft's streaming fuselage. That Beurling's relish in the public recounting of this tale may be pure bravado is attested to by his brother, who told biographer Brian Nolan that the incident left the flier with tearful nightmares ever after.

There are plenty of tears in the war's aftermath as well. Peter Townsend tells of a captured Luftwaffe bombardier who breaks down when told his incendiaries killed several families, and in *Harvest of Messerschmitts* Dennis Knight recounts an ironic story about Professor Hassel von Wedel, the official Luftwaffe historian, who on a rare Messerschmitt flight over Maidstone is shot down by a Hurricane and crashes into a farm building, killing the farmer's wife and four-year-old daughter: "The Professor was so distraught at what he'd done that he wandered about with tears in his eyes trying to apologize and was finally led away" (p. 134). The endurance of human sympathy is tested in the bombing war but prevails against appalling odds. In *The Diving Eagle* Peter Stahl undertakes few missions without expressing pity for the victims below. One of the more surprising revelations of this Junkers 88 pilot's memoirs is that the Belgian and Dutch people working at captured bases, although having no allegiance to Germany, can nevertheless feel sympathy for the German filers they serve at mess. Even Dresden, soon to be destroyed in the most controversial British and American raid of the war, reacts generously to an earlier light attack on its railway yards, in which some Allied prisoners of war are killed, by giving them the honor of a full military funeral. Four weeks later up to a quarter million Dresdeners would be denied burial in favor of mass pyres.

Matters on the ground are what spoil things for the fliers. Readers may accept the idealism of these memoirists or question the naïveté of such a perspective. Can the business of a Junkers 88 over London or a Lancaster over Hamburg be completely insulated from the holocaust unleashed below? And can the combat of a Jagdstaffel and a Spitfire squadron over Kent in 1940 or of Heinz Knoke's Messerschmitt and an unnamed tall American's Thunderbolt in the skies above Brunswick in 1944 be considered totally apart from the remaking of the political map of the world beneath them? Their countries' leaders would certainly not think so, and there is a strong reciprocity between the images these airmen have of themselves and the way their national leaders fashion those images into effective rallying points for the war.

Can a World War II airman be immune to such uses not only of his trade but of its mystique as well? For all its demands of expertise and courage this era's flying bred a certain amount of little-boyishness which memoirists find charming to recall and even necessary to complete the image. An oddly recurrent scene tells much about this exuberantly boyish style. In *Mosquito Victory* Jack Currie finds himself stranded at a railway station with hours to wait between trains when a friendly signalman offers to halt an express and let Currie ride in the engineer's cab. The elated flier is soon off on a long-dreamed-of journey, taking the controls and sounding the train's whistle as it rockets through the night at a thirty miles per hour more thrilling than in his Mosquito at fifteen times that speed. The experience repeats itself in *Enemy Coast Ahead* when Guy Gibson rides in another engine cab and is more taken with its size and power than with that of his Lancaster over the Ruhr. The final proof of universality, in which opposing airmen share each other's roles and sympathies, happens in the Ruhr itself on the night of December 23, 1944, when Messerschmitt pilot Heinz Knoke makes his way home in the locomotive cab of a freight train bound for Bremen—like his RAF counterparts, having the time of his life.

Sounding the whistle of a speeding train is surely not the most telling instance of behavior in their finest hours, but its coincidence among these memoirs brings the participants closer together than their most intimate moments in the air, where their weapons form a fatal separation, or in hospital or prisoner-of-war scenes later, where there is the rude presence of a blown-off limb or a guard's pistol to remind one of the facts. In those cases all the codes and gestures spoke a sometimes desperate message: I, a flier, am really just like you, and so as we fight, let us act with mercy and respect. In their railway cabs, back on solid earth, where man has sped and whistled to his heart's content for all the years since creation, these adventurers can thrill just as much in more familiar dimensions of human daring. Their hours in the air would soon elapse; in the next war air combat would break through the sound barrier and after that to the edge of space, where opposing airships would appear as electronic symbols on a scope. Even as that age beckons—and nearly every writer sees it coming as he ends his memoir—the adolescent dreams of speed and power back on earth make their strong appeal, and the brief interval of man-to-man fighting over the skies of England and Europe passes as if it had never happened at all.

Bibliography

PAGE REFERENCES in the text are to the editions cited below. When page references are not to the first edition, the year of first publication follows in brackets.

Andrews, Allen. *The Air Marshals.* New York: William Morrow, 1970.

Baumbach, Werner. *Broken Swastika: The Defeat of the Luftwaffe.* London: Robert Hale, 1986 [1949].

Beaman, John R., Jr. *Messerschmitt Bf109 in Action.* Carrollton, Tex.: Squadron/Signal, 1983.

Bennett, D. C. T. *Pathfinder.* London: Goodall Publications, 1983 [1958].

Berenbrok, Hans Dieter [Cajus Becker, pseud.]. *The Luftwaffe War Diaries.* Garden City, N.Y.: Doubleday, 1967 [1964].

Bishop, Edward. *Hurricane.* Shrewsbury: Airlife, 1986.

Bowman, Gerald. *War in the Air.* London: Evans Brothers, 1956.

Bowyer, Michael J. F. *The Spitfire 50 Years On.* Wellingborough: Patrick Stephens, 1986.

Braddon, Russell. *Cheshire V. C.* London: Evans Brothers, 1954.

Braham, J. R. D. "Bob." *"Scramble!"* London: William Kimber, 1985 [1961].

Brickhill, Paul. *The Dam Busters.* New York: Ballantine, 1955 [1951].

———. *Reach for the Sky: The Story of Douglas Bader.* London: Fontana/Collins, 1985 [1954 as *Fight for the Sky*].

Burns, Michael. *Spitfire! Spitfire!* Poole: Blandford, 1986.

Burt, Kendall, and James Leasor. *The One That Got Away.* London: Collins with Michael Joseph, 1956.

Charlwood, Don. *No Moon Tonight.* London: Goodall Publications, 1984 [1956].

Cheshire, Leonard. *Bomber Pilot.* London: Hutchinson, 1943.

Closterman, Pierre. *The Big Show.* New York: Ballantine, 1958 [1951].

Cross, Roy, Gerald Scarborough, and Hans Ebert. *Messerschmitt Bf109: Versions B-E.* Cambridge: Patrick Stephens, 1972.

Currie, Jack. *The Augsburg Raid.* London: Goodall Publications, 1987.

———. *Lancaster Target.* London: Goodall Publications, 1981 [1977].

———. *Mosquito Victory.* London: Goodall Publications, 1983.

Deere, Alan C. *Nine Lives.* London: Coronet/Hodder Fawcett, 1961 [1959].

Deighton, Len. *Fighter.* London: Jonathan Cape, 1977.

Dudgeon, A. G. *The Luck of the Devil.* Shrewsbury: Airlife, 1985.

Flack, Jeremy. *Spitfire: A Living Legend.* London: Osprey, 1985.

Galland, Adolf. *The First and the Last*. New York: Henry Holt, 1954.

Garbett, Mike, and Brian Goulding. *Lancaster at War: 3*. London: Ian Allan, 1984.

Gibson, Guy. *Enemy Coast Ahead*. London: Goodall Publications, 1986 [1946].

Gleave, Tom [R. A. F. Casualty]. *I Had a Row With a German*. London: Macmillan, 1941.

Golley, John. *The Day of the Typhoon*. Wellingborough: Patrick Stephens, 1986.

Harris, Arthur. *Bomber Offensive*. London: Collins, 1947.

Henshaw, Alex. *Sigh for a Merlin*. London: John Murray, 1979.

Hillary, Richard. *The Last Enemy*. New York: St. Martin's, 1983 [1942 as *Falling Through Space*].

Johnen, Wilhelm. *Duel Under the Stars*. London: William Kimber, 1957.

Johnson, J. E. *Wing Leader*. New York: Ballantine, 1957 [1956].

Knight, Dennis. *Harvest of Messerschmitts: The Chronicle of a Village at War*. London: Frederick Warne/Leo Cooper, 1981.

Knoke, Heinz. *I Flew for the Führer*. New York: Henry Holt, 1954 [1953].

McKee, Alexander. *Dresden 1945: The Devil's Tinderbox*. London: Souvenir, 1982.

McRoberts, Douglas. *Lions Rampant: The Story of 602 Spitfire Squadron*. London: William Kimber, 1985.

Monks, Noel. *Squadrons Up!* New York: Whittlesley House/McGraw-Hill, 1942.

Munson, Kenneth. *German Aircraft of World War 2*. Poole: Blandford, 1978.

Nolan, Brian. *Hero: The Falcon of Malta*. Edinburgh: William Blackwood, 1982 [1981].

Offenberg, Jean. *Lonely Warrior: The Journal of Battle of Britain Fighter Pilot Jean Offenberg*. Edited by Victor Houart. London: Souvenir, 1956.

Orange, Vincent. *Sir Keith Park*. London: Methuen, 1984.

Oxspring, Bobby. *Spitfire Command*. London: Grafton, 1987 [1984].

Quill, Jeffrey. *Birth of a Legend: The Spitfire*. London: Quiller, 1986.

————. *Spitfire*. London: John Murray, 1983.

Ramsey, Winston G., ed. *The Battle of Britain Then and Now*. London: After the Battle/Battle of Britain Prints, 1985 [1980].

Rawnsley, C. F., and Robert Wright. *Night Fighter*. London: Collins, 1957.

Richards, Denis, and Hilary St. G. Saunders. *Royal Air Force 1939–1945*. 3 vol. London: Her Majesty's Stationery Office, 1953–1954.

Riley, Gordon. *Spitfire Survivors*. Bourne End: Aston, 1984.

Rudel, Hans Ulrich. *Stuka Pilot*. New York: Ballantine, 1958 [1950].

Saward, Dudley. *"Bomber" Harris*. London: Cassell, 1984.

Sawyer, Tom. *Only Owls and Bloody Fools Fly at Night*. London: Goodall Publications, 1985 [1982].

Scutts, Jerry. *Hurricane in Action.* Carrollton, Tex.: Squadron/Signal, 1986.

Smith, Ron. *Rear Gunner Pathfinders.* London: Goodall Publications, 1987.

Stahl, Peter. *The Diving Eagle.* London: William Kimber, 1984 [1978].

Taylor, Geoff. *Piece of Cake.* London: Peter Davies, 1956.

Terraine, John. *The Right of the Line: The Royal Air Force in the European War.* London: Hodder and Stoughton, 1985.

Thompson, Walter. *Lancaster to Berlin.* London: Goodall, 1985.

Townsend, Peter. *Duel in the Dark.* London: Harrap, 1986.

_____. *Duel of Eagles.* New York: Simon and Schuster, 1970.

Tripp, Miles. *The Eighth Passenger.* London: Macmillan, 1985 [1969].

Index